present

TOUCH

by **VICKY JONES**

Touch was commissioned by Soho Theatre and was first
performed at Soho Theatre, London, on 6 July 2017

TOUCH

by VICKY JONES

CAST

DEE	**Amy Morgan**
EDDIE	**James Marlowe**
VERA	**Naana Agyei-Ampadu**
MILES	**James Clyde**
PADDY	**Edward Bluemel**
SAM	**Matthew Aubrey**

CREATIVE TEAM

Director	**Vicky Jones**
Set and Costume Designer	**ULTZ**
Lighting Designer	**Richard Howell**
Sound Designer	**Isobel Waller-Bridge**
Associate Sound Designer	**Harry Johnson**
Dramaturg	**Phoebe Waller-Bridge**
Movement Director	**Polly Bennett**
Costume Supervisor	**Claire Wardroper**
Production Manager	**Simon MacColl**
Assistant Director	**Lakesha Arie Angelo**
Casting Director	**Nadine Rennie** CDG
Company Stage Manager	**Felix Dunning**
Deputy Stage Manager	**Olivia Kerslake**
Assistant Stage Manager	**Cáit Canavan**

CAST

AMY MORGAN | DEE

Amy Morgan's theatre credits include: *Travesties* (Menier Chocolate Factory/West End); *Red Velvet* (Kenneth Branagh Company at Garrick Theatre); *The Beaux Stratagem* (National Theatre); *The Broken Heart* (Shakespeare's Globe); *An Ideal Husband* (Chichester); *Once a Catholic* (Royal Court Liverpool); *A Christmas Carol* (Royal Festival Hall); *Once a Catholic* (Tricycle); *Trelawny of the Wells* (Donmar Warehouse); *The Country Wife* (Royal Exchange); *Hay Fever* (Noël Coward); *Inadmissible Evidence* (Donmar Warehouse); *The Taming of the Shrew, Blackthorn, Flora's War, To Kill a Mockingbird* (Theatr Clwyd); *Deepcut* (Sherman Cymru). Film and television credits include: *Pan* (Warner Brothers); *Mr Selfridge, A Way of Life, The Great War* (ITV); *Live At The Electric, Father Brown, Holby City, Baker Boys, Crash* (BBC); *Love Matters* (Sky); *The Royal* (YTV) and the pilots of *Modern Medicine* (Fremantle Media) and *Break* (Ben Steel Films). Radio 4 credits include: *The Eustace Diamonds, Deep Cut* and *Lemon Meringue Pie.*

JAMES MARLOWE | EDDIE

James Marlowe trained at LAMDA. His theatre credits include: *The Play That Goes Wrong* (West End/Australian tour); *Waiting for Waiting for Godot* (St James); *Peter Pan Goes Wrong* (UK tour); *Macbeth* (Mercury); *Primetime* (Royal Court); *The Man Who Shot Liberty Valance* (Park); *Capitalism is Crisis* (Arcola); *Blue Man Group* (NYC, Boston & US national tour); *The Bunker Trilogy* (world tour); *The Captive* (Finborough); *The London Cuckolds* (Pleasance); *When We Meet Again* (BAC). Television credits include: *Teenage Tommies* (BBC). James also played 'Walter' in the viral comedy hit *The Expert*. James is Creative Director of Tucked In Productions. www.tuckedin.co.uk

NAANA AGYEI-AMPADU | VERA

Naana Agyei-Ampadu's theatre credits include: *Fury* (Soho); *I Want My Hat Back, The Amen Corner, A Pacifist's Guide to the War on Cancer* (with Complicite and HOME Manchester), *Caroline or Change* (National Theatre); *The Oresteia, Measure for Measure, The Frontline* (Shakespeare's Globe); *Feast, Been So Long* (Young Vic); *Little Shop of Horrors* (New Wolsey, Ipswich); *Avenue Q* (Noël Coward). Television credits include: *Hard Sun* (BBC); *Cuffs* (Tiger Aspect for BBC); *The Future Wags of Great Britain* (Channel 4). She played Elaine in debbie tucker green's *Gone* (BBC Radio 3) and starred in Steven Spielberg's *Ready Player One* (Warner Bros).

JAMES CLYDE | MILES

James Clyde's theatre credits include: *In the Depths of Dead Love* (Print Room); *Cymbeline, King Lear,* Mr Wormwood in *Matilda, Romeo and Juliet, Days of Significance* (with Tricycle), *Comedy of Errors, Twelfth Night* (RSC); *The God of Carnage, School for Wives* (Nuffield); *Dangerous Lady* (Theatre Royal Stratford East); *The Illusion* (Southwark Playhouse); *Hamlet, The Art of Random Whistling* (Young Vic); *Jane Eyre* (Shared Experience/Young Vic); *As You Like It, Hedda Gabler, Tobaccoland, The Candidate, Misfits, The Tempest, A Taste of Honey, Macbeth* (Manchester Royal Exchange); *Twelfth Night* (National Theatre); *Single Spies* (Watermill); *Macbeth* (Shakespeare's Globe); *Caucasian Chalk Circle, Jane Eyre, After Mrs Rochester* (Shared Experience); *The Sea at Night* (Hackney Empire); *Absolute Beginners* (Lyric, Hammersmith); *A Model Girl* (Greenwich Theatre); *I Just Stopped By To See The Man* (Octagon); *Ying Tong* (West Yorkshire Playhouse/West End/BBC Radio); *The Lucky Ones, The Eleventh Commandment, A Going Concern* (Hampstead); *The Ecstatic Bible* (Adelaide Festival); *Scenes from an Execution* (Barbican/tour); *Dreaming* (Queens); *The Castle* (Riverside Studios/tour); *Home Free* (Finborough); *Resistance, Mr Thomas* (Old Red Lion); *Hated Nightfall, Wounds to the Face* (Royal Court); *Jack's Out* (Bush); *A Hard Heart, All For Love* (Almeida); *The Gentleman From Olmedo* (Gate); *The White Devil* (Cockpit). Film credits include: *Beauty, Anonymous, The Honeytrap, Cheese, Croupier, Your Night Tonight, Prick Up Your Ears, Glitch.* Television credits include: *Leonardo, New Tricks, Between the Lines, Back Up, The Stairwell* (BBC); *Above Suspicion: Deadly Intent* (La Plante Productions); *The Bill* (Talkback Thames); *Boudicca* (ITV); *London Bridge* (Carlton); *Mr Thomas* (Channel 4); *Made in Heaven, Cluedo, Maigret, In Suspicious Circumstances* (Granada).

EDWARD BLUEMEL | PADDY

Edward Bluemel graduated from the Royal Welsh College of Music and Drama and was named the Winner (Highly Commended Prize) of the prestigious Spotlight Prize for acting in 2015. He made his debut feature film performance in *Access All Areas* as the lead character of Heath and shot Jaume Collet-Serra's upcoming action-thriller film, *The Commuter* with Liam Neeson. Edward was recently seen playing Jacob Hamilton in new drama *The Halcyon* for ITV and is currently starring in *Love in Idleness* alongside Eve Best and Anthony Hamilton at London's Apollo Theatre on the West End.

MATTHEW AUBREY | SAM

Matthew Aubrey's theatre credits include: *Future Conditional* (Old Vic); *Pride and Prejudice* (Sheffield Theatre); *Under Milk Wood* (Unterberg Poetry Centre, NYC); *A Life of Galileo* (RSC/Birmingham Rep); *A Radicalisation of Bradley Manning* (National Theatre of Wales); *A Life of Galileo, Boris Gudanov, The Orphan of Zhao* (RSC); *The Passion* (National Theatre of Wales) and *War Horse* (National Theatre). Film and television credits include: *Just Jim* (Vox Pictures) and *Made in Dagenham* (Number 9 Films); *Bang* (S4C); *Kiss Me First* (E4/Netflix); *Mum, Privates, Gracie, The Passing Bells, Framed* (BBC); *Black Mirror: Yuletide* (Channel 4); *The Indian Doctor* (Rondo Media); *Birdsong* (Working Title/BBC) and *The Sinking of The Laconia* (Talkback Thames).

CREATIVE TEAM

VICKY JONES | DIRECTOR
Vicky Jones is co-Founder and co-Artistic Director of DryWrite with Phoebe Waller-Bridge.

As a director, Vicky's credits include the multi award-winning production of *Fleabag* (Edinburgh Festival Fringe/Soho/UK and international tours); *Mydidae* by Jack Thorne (Soho/Trafalgar Studios); *The Tour Guide* by James Graham, *Separated* by Sara Masters (iceandfire/UK tour) and *The Freedom of the City* by Brian Friel (Finborough).

The One, Vicky's first play as a writer, won the 2013 Verity Bargate Award before its world premiere at London's Soho Theatre. Vicky is currently under commission as a writer for the National Theatre and for several TV companies including the BBC, Sid Gentle and Leopard Drama. She has co-written a one-off drama with Stephen Merchant (*The Office*, *Extras*). She is also writing a new drama-comedy for Entertainment One.

ULTZ | SET AND COSTUME DESIGNER
ULTZ began his career as an actor and drama teacher and has also worked as a director. Since graduating from the Central School of Speech and Drama in 1970 he has worked worldwide in theatre, opera and with Urban Music.

Recent designs include sets and costumes for: *One Love – the Bob Marley musical* (Birmingham Rep); *Ma Rainey's Black Bottom* (National Theatre); *Ariodante* (Canadian Opera Company); *Torn* (Royal Court); *La Musica* (Young Vic); *Gloriana* (Royal Opera House); *The River* (Broadway) and *Boy* (Almeida, costumes only). At the Royal Court ULTZ designed the first productions of plays by Tarell Alvin McCraney, Jez Butterworth, Roy Williams, Bola Agbaje, Rachel Delahey and John Donnelly.

As an Associate Artist at Theatre Royal Stratford East, he develops and directs new pieces of Urban Music Theatre including: Jean Genet's play *The Blacks Remixed*; *Da Boyz* (a hip hop version of *The Boys from Syracuse*); with Blue Boy Entertainment, *Pied Piper – a hip hop dance revolution* (also Barbican/UK tour). He was part of the creative team for the stage version of *The Harder They Come* (also Barbican/West End/Toronto).

ULTZ won a Tony Award nomination and an Olivier Award for set design for *Jerusalem* (Royal Court/West End/Broadway) and an Off-West End Award for set design for *The Beauty Queen of Leenane* (Young Vic). *Ma Rainey's Black Bottom* won the Olivier Award for Best Revival 2016. *Pied Piper* won an Olivier Award for Outstanding Achievement in an Affiliate Theatre.

RICHARD HOWELL I LIGHTING DESIGNER

Richard Howell's theatre credits include *Jekyll and Hyde* (Old Vic); *The Homecoming*, *Eastis East* (Trafalgar Studios for Jamie Lloyd Company); *Privacy* (Donmar Warehouse/Public Theater, New York); *Bad Jews* (Theatre Royal Bath/West End/UK tour); *Labyrinth* (Hampstead); *Breaking the Code, A Doll's House, Little Shop of Horrors* (Manchester Royal Exchange); *The Wild Party* (The Other Palace); *The Glass Menagerie* (Headlong/UK tour); *I See You* (Royal Court, Jerwood Theatre Upstairs); *Playing for Time* (Sheffield Crucible); *The Grinning Man, The Crucible, The Life and Times of Fanny Hill* (Bristol Old Vic); *Plastic, 4000 Miles* (Ustinov, Bath); *Guards at The Taj, The Invisible* (Bush); *Project Polunin* (Sadler's Wells); *Il Trittico, Flight, Madame Butterfly* and *La Fanciulla* (Opera Holland Park).

ISOBEL WALLER-BRIDGE I SOUND DESIGNER

Isobel Waller-Bridge's theatre credits include: *The Seven Acts of Mercy, Hecuba* (RSC +); *Three Sisters* (Lyric, Belfast ++); *The Philanderer* (Orange Tree ++); *Dutchman* (Young Vic ++); *The End of Longing* (Playhouse ++); *The Damned United* (West Yorkshire Playhouse ++); *Kite* (Soho ++); *By the Bog of Cats* (Abbey ++); *The One That Got Away, Exit the King* (Ustinov ++); *The Hook* (Royal & Derngate +); *Hope Place* (Liverpool Everyman +); *King Lear* (Chichester Festival Theatre/BAM +); *Neville's Island* (Chichester Festival Theatre/West End +); *If Only* (Minerva +); *Billy Liar, Orlando, So Here We Are* (Manchester Royal Exchange ++); *Posh* (Nottingham Playhouse/ Salisbury ++); *Uncle Vanya* (St James ++); *Incognito* (Bush ++; Off West End Award for Best Sound Design); *Not the Worst Place* (Sherman Cymru ++); *Yellow Face* (National Theatre ++); *Lampedusa, Fleabag, The Girl with the Iron Claws, Blink* (Soho ++); the Ideal World season (Watford Palace Theatre ++); *Forever House* (Theatre Royal Plymouth ++); *Sleuth* (Watermill ++); *Mydidae* (Traverse/West End ++); *Gruesome Playground Injuries* (Gate ++).

Film, TV and radio composition includes: *Fleabag* (BBC); Additional Music for *War & Peace* (BBC/Weinstein Company); *James* (dir. Claire Oakley, Winner Best Composer Underwire Film Festival); *Tracks* (dir. Claire Oakley); *The Frozen Planet: Making Of* (BBC); *Secret Symphony* (Samsung/The Times); *Gilead* (Radio 3); *Physics* (dir. Claire Oakley, Winner BFI Best Film Best of Boroughs).

Credits as Musical Director: *The Boy I Love* (V&A); *A Woman Killed With Kindness* (National Theatre) and *A Christmas Carol* (Lowry).

+ Composer ++ Composer and Sound Designer

LAKESHA ARIE-ANGELO I ASSISTANT DIRECTOR

Lakesha Arie-Angelo is Soho Theatre's Resident Director and was Assistant Director on its recent musical *Roller Diner*. Previous directing: *AS:NT* (Theatre503) as part of Rapid Write; *Prodigal* (Bush) for 'Artistic Directors of the Future Black Lives: Black Words'. Scratch of *Sugar, Rum, Molasses* (The CLF Theatre) as writer and director. As Resident Assistant Director at Finborough Theatre: *P'Yongyang, Treasure* and Vibrant 2015 Festival of Finborough Playwrights. During the residency, Lakesha was awarded the Richard Carne Trust sponsorship.

DryWrite is a multi award-winning and Olivier-nominated new-writing theatre company that challenges writers to work with specific briefs and goals to actively engage audiences with argument and action.

Founded in 2007, DryWrite has since worked with over one hundred playwrights. They have produced original work for theatres including Soho Theatre, Roundhouse, York Theatre Royal, Hampstead Theatre, Trafalgar Studios and Latitude Festival, and have toured throughout the UK and internationally.

They are currently an associate company of Soho Theatre. DryWrite is made up of Co-Artistic Directors Vicky Jones and Phoebe Waller-Bridge, Producer Francesca Moody and Stage Manager Charlotte McBrearty.

www.drywrite.com | www.facebook.com/drywrite | @DryWrite

Thanks

DryWrite would like to thank the following individuals and organisations without whom this production would not have been possible: Steve Marmion and all at Soho Theatre, Fi McCurdy, Marina Dixon and all at Underbelly, IdeasTap, Ben Gregory, Adrian Wheeler, Teresa Waller-Bridge, Al Smith, Will Oldroyd, Chloé Nelkin, Richard Lakos, Conor Woodman, Tania Harrison, Mirain Jones, Francesca Tortora, Workspace and everyone who contributed to our Kickstarter, with special thanks to Matthew Steer, Lindsay Duncan, Stephen Daly, Richard Corgan, Katie Beard, Michael Elwyn, Rory Hudson, Jack Thorne, Martin Adams and Gilly McDonald, Peter Moody, Tom Salinsky and Deborah Francis-White, Martin French, Kevin McNally, Susan Shenkman, and Olivia Colman.

Supporters of DryWrite

DryWrite relies on the generosity of its audiences, friends and patrons without whom it would not be possible to continue making the work we do. We are truly grateful to all of our supporters and would love you to join them. For more information on our **friends and patrons scheme** and how to give please visit our website at **www.drywrite.com.**

FRIENDS Michael Elwyn, Rory Hudson, Jack Thorne

BRONZE PATRONS Martin Adams, Peter Moody, Martin French,Tom Salinsky and Deborah Francis-White

SILVER PATRONS Kevin McNally, Susan Shenkman, Olivia Colman

Soho Theatre is London's most vibrant venue for new theatre, comedy and cabaret. We occupy a unique and vital place in the British cultural landscape. Our mission is to produce new work, discover and nurture new writers and artists, and target and develop new audiences. We work with artists in a variety of ways, from full producing of new plays, to co-producing new work, working with associate artists and presenting the best new emerging theatre companies that we can find.

We have numerous artists on attachment and under commission, including Soho Six and a thriving Young Company of writers and comedy groups. We read and see hundreds of scripts and shows a year.

'the place was buzzing, and there were queues all over the building as audiences waited to go into one or other of the venue's spaces....young, exuberant and clearly anticipating a good time.' Guardian.

We attract over 240,000 audience members a year at Soho Theatre, at festivals and through our national and international touring. We produced, co-produced or staged over 35 new plays in the last 12 months.

As an entrepreneurial charity and social enterprise, we have created an innovative and sustainable business model. We maximise value from Arts Council England and philanthropic funding, contributing more to government in tax and NI than we receive in public funding.

Registered Charity No: 267234

Soho Theatre, 21 Dean Street
London W1D 3NE
Admin 020 7287 5060
Box Office 020 7478 0100

Supported using public funding by
ARTS COUNCIL
ENGLAND

OPPORTUNITIES FOR WRITERS AT SOHO THEATRE

We are looking for unique and unheard voices – from all backgrounds, attitudes and places.

We want to make things you've never seen before.

Alongside workshops, readings and notes sessions, there are several ways writers can connect with Soho Theatre. You can

- **enter** our prestigious biennial competition the **Verity Bargate Award** just as **Vicky Jones** did in 2013 with her Award-winning first play The One.

- **participate** in our nine month long **Writers' Labs programme**, where we will take you through a three-draft process.

- **submit** your script to submissions@sohotheatre.com where your play will go directly to our Artistic team

- **invite** us to see your show via coverage@sohotheatre.com

We consider every submission for production or any of the further development opportunities.

sohotheatre.com

Keep up to date:

sohotheatre.com/mailing-list
@sohotheatre all social media

DEVELOPMENT AND DONORS

Soho Theatre is a charity and social enterprise. We are supported by Arts Council England and we put every £1 donated back into our work. Our supporters are key to our success and we are immensely grateful for their support. We would like to thank all our supporters for their generosity:

Principal Supporters
Nicholas Allott
Hani Farsi
Jack and Linda Keenan
Amelia and Neil Mendoza
Lady Susie Sainsbury
Carolyn Ward
Jennifer and Roger Wingate

The Soho Circle
Celia Atkin
Jo Bennett-Coles
Moyra Doyle
Stephen Garrett
Hedley and Fiona Goldberg
Jon Grant
Tim Macready
Suzanne Pirret

Corporate Supporters
Adnams Southwold
Bargate Murray
Bates Wells & Braithwaite
Cameron Mackintosh Ltd
Character Seven
EPIC Private Equity
Financial Express
Fosters
The Groucho Club
John Lewis Oxford Street
Latham & Watkins LLP
Lionsgate UK
The Nadler Hotel
Oberon Books Ltd
Overbury Leisure
Quo Vadis
Richmond Associates
Soho Estates
Soundcraft

Trusts & Foundations
Backstage Trust
Bertha Foundation
Bruce Wake Charitable Trust
Chapman Charitable Trust
Cockayne – Grants for the Arts and
   The London Community Foundation
Esmée Fairbairn Foundation
Foyle Foundation
Fidelio Charitable Trust
Garrick Charitable Trust
Harold Hyam Wingate Foundation
Hyde Park Place Estate Charity
John Ellerman Foundation
JP Getty Jnr Charitable Trust
Mohamed S. Farsi Foundation
Santander Foundation
St Giles-in-the-Fields and William
   Shelton Educational Charity

The Andor Charitable Trust
The Austin and Hope Pilkington
   Charitable Trust
The Boris Karloff Charitable Foundation
The Charles Rifkind and Jonathan Levy
   Charitable Settlement
The Charlotte Bonham-Carter
   Charitable Trust
The John S. Cohen Foundation
The Ernest Cook Trust
The Edward Harvist Trust
The Goldsmiths' Company
The Ian Mactaggart Trust
The Idlewild Trust
The John Thaw Foundation
The Kobler Trust
The Mackintosh Foundation
The Peggy Ramsay Foundation
The Rose Foundation
The Royal Victoria Hall Foundation
The St James's Piccadilly Charity
The Teale Charitable Trust
The Theatres Trust
The Thistle Trust
The Wolfson Foundation
Unity Theatre Charitable Trust

Soho Theatre Best Friends
Matthew and Brooke Barzun
Nick Bowers
Prof Dr Niels Brabandt
Barbara Broccoli
Richard Collins
David and Beverly Cox
Miranda Curtis
Isobel and Michael Holland
Beatrice Hollond
David King
Lady Caroline Mactaggart
Hannah Pierce
Amy Ricker
Ian Ritchie and Jocelyne van den Bossche
Ann Stanton
Alex Vogel
Sian and Matthew Westerman
Mark Whiteley
Gary Wilder
Alexandra Williams
Hilary and Stuart Williams

Soho Theatre Dear Friends
Nick Allan
Christiane Amanpour
Ken Anderson
David Aukin
Natalie Bakova
James Boyle
Rajan Brotia
James Brown

Simon Brown, Founder The ESTAS Group
Lisa Bryer
Steve Coogan
Fiona Dewar
Cherry and Rob Dickins
Manu Duggal
Chris Evans
Denzil and Renate Fernandez
Dominic Flynn
Jonathan Glanz and Manuela Raimondo
Alban Gordon
Kate Horton
Fawn James
John James
Dede Johnston
Shappi Khorsandi
Jeremy King
Lynne Kirwin
Michael Kunz
David and Linda Lakhdhir
Anita and Brook Land
Jonathan Levy
Patrick Marber
Nick Mason and Annette Lynton Mason
Aoife O'Brien
Adam Morley
Aoife O'Brien
Rick Pappas
Natasha Parker
Leanne Pollock
Lauren Prakke
Phil and Jane Radcliff
John Reid
James Robertson
Sue Robertson
Alexandra Sears
Robert & Melanie Stoutzker
Dominic and Ali Wallis
Garry Watts
Gregg Wilson
Andrea Wong
Matt Woodford
Henry Wyndham
Christopher Yu

Soho Theatre Good Friends
Oladipo Agboluaje
James Atkinson
Jonathan and Amanda Baines
Uri Baruchin
Antonio Batista
Alex Bridport
Jesse Buckle
Indigo Carnie
Paul Carpenter
Chris Carter
Sharon Eva Degen
Michelle Dietz
Niki di Palma
Jeff Dormer
Geoffrey and Janet Eagland
Edwina Ellis
Peter Fenwick
Gail and Michael Flesch
Sue Fletcher
James Flitton

Cyrus Gilbert-Rolfe
Eva Greenspan
Doug Hawkins
Etan Ilfeld
John Ireland
Fran Jones
Eric Knopp
Susie Lea
Simon Lee
Tom Levi
Ian Livingston
Nicola Martin
Kathryn Marten
Amanda Mason
Neil Mastrarrigo
Robert McFarland
Gerry McGrail
Andrew and Jane McManus
Mr and Mrs Roger Myddelton
Dr Tara Naidoo
Max Nicholson
Alan Pardoe
Nick Pontt
Edward Pivcevic
Sadia Quyam
Stephanie Ressort
Barry Serjent
Ed Smith
Hari Sriskantha
Francis and Marie-Claude Stobart
Sam Swallow
Lesley Symons
Sue Terry
Gabriel Vogt
Anja Weise
Mike Welsh
Matt Whitehurst
Allan Willis
Liz Young

We would also like to thank those supporters who wish to remain anonymous.

Soho Theatre has the support of the Channel 4 Playwrights' Scheme sponsored by Channel 4 Television.

We are also supported by Westminster City Council West End Ward Budget and the London Borough of Waltham Forest.

This list is correct as of March 2017.

The production would like to thank Ronnie's Flowers of Berwick Street and Bargain Beds Superstore.

TOUCH

Vicky Jones

Acknowledgements

Thank you to Phoebe Waller-Bridge, Char McBrearty, Francesca Moody, Phil Porter, Steven Poole, Gabriel Bisset-Smith, Robert Cawsey. Thank you to my family. Also thanks so much to all at Soho Theatre for their tireless faith and hard work, especially Adam Brace, David Luff, Nadine Rennie, Steve Marmion, Kelly Fogarty, Sophie Coke-Steel, Charlotte Bennett and Mark Godfrey. Thanks to Sarah Liisa Wilkinson and all at Nick Hern Books. And thanks to the cast and stage management of *Touch* for their contribution towards the development of the script during rehearsals, and for their patience.

V.J.

For Steven Poole

Characters

DEE
EDDIE
VERA
MILES
PADDY
SAM

Note on Text

A forward slash (/) indicates an overlap.

A dash (–) indicates an interruption.

A space on the text indicates a beat or a pause. The length of the pause is indicated by the length of space in the text.

This text went to press before the end of rehearsals and so may differ slightly from the play as performed.

1. Eddie 1

DEE*'s flat is tiny and resembles a ramshackle bedsit, though it has a small bathroom attached with a shower, sink and toilet. The room is full of her clutter and every surface and corner is filled with something. There is a cooking area with no sink, but with a fridge and a hob, with pans stacked on top. There is an old wheelie office chair. There is a bookshelf containing self-help books and feminist literature as well as fiction. There is a wardrobe with her clothes pouring out of the front. There is a pile of unopened mail. There are empty wine bottles, dirty cups and glasses. There is a pan in the shower. There is a stepper exercise machine. There is a full rubbish bag in the corner.*

DEE *is trying to tidy up.* EDDIE*'s back is turned. Suddenly he turns around to look at her.*

DEE   No!

EDDIE   What the hell is this place?

DEE   You were supposed to wait outside while I tidied.

EDDIE   You live here?

DEE   There's not really room for all my stuff.

EDDIE   You might find there's room at the back of your cupboards, if you –

DEE   You don't know what you're talking about.

EDDIE   I'm impressed you've managed to get it into this state in what – three weeks?

DEE   Amazing what you can do if you put your mind to it.

           She poses in some mess.

EDDIE   You remind me of, what are they called? A Manic Pixie Dream Girl.

DEE   Ugh I hated that film.

EDDIE   I thought you'd love that kind of thing.

DEE   Ugh, I can't stand those self-satisfied, ironic, 'indie' movies, about flighty male-fantasy women who just say the kookiest, most adorable things and are constantly falling over and fucking skipping and...

EDDIE   Easy.

DEE   They offend me.

EDDIE   Right.

DEE   I feel contempt for them.

EDDIE   I can tell.
               Chill out.

               DEE laughs suddenly, embarrassed.

               She grabs a takeaway that EDDIE *is holding and puts it in the fridge.*

DEE   Thank you for dinner by the way.

EDDIE   No problem.

DEE   You sure you don't want any of this?

EDDIE   You keep it.

DEE   I've got next time.

EDDIE   So there's gonna be a next time?

DEE   Of course!

               DEE moves towards him. They kiss. But she stops him, pushes him back on the bed. He resists.

EDDIE   What you doing?

DEE   Not what you think...

She selects some music.

You ever been to a strip club, Eddie?
Don't say yes by the way.

EDDIE   Well that's easy because I never have.

DEE   Would you like to?

EDDIE   I would if you were the only dancer.
            You're beautiful.

DEE   Shit business model though, Eddie. Only one
            dancer.

EDDIE   Okay.

            DEE *is doing a sort of good lap dance.*

DEE   I'm good at this.

EDDIE   I can see.

            *She dances towards him and then tries to get his
            cock out.*

            Steady – alright.
            So that's gotta be out then, does it?

            *He gets his cock out himself, though it's masked by
            his hand and trousers.*

DEE   Relax. Enjoy yourself.

            DEE *continues the dance, sort of giggling, but
            trying really hard to be provocative and exciting,
            striking a pose and throwing her head back to
            look at him seductively.*

            *She continues to make half-ironic, sexy-sounding
            noises as she dances.*

            Sexy sexy sexy… Lalalalaaaa…Uh uh uh uh uh…

            The music steps up and DEE *steps up her dancing
            accordingly. She indicates that* EDDIE *should
            continue wanking. He reluctantly obliges.*

EDDIE   STOP.

         DEE *stops dancing*.

DEE   What?

EDDIE   Stop. Don't move.

DEE   (*Giggles*.) Like this?

EDDIE   Turn the music off.

DEE   Wow okay.

         She does.

         What?

         Beat.

EDDIE   A mouse just ran under that pile of pants.

DEE   Oh did it?

EDDIE   You know you have a mouse here?

DEE   Well I thought I might have heard something –

         EDDIE *strides into the bathroom and comes out
         again with some scrunched-up tissue*.

EDDIE   Where is it?

         DEE *pisses herself laughing at* EDDIE.

DEE   What d'you reckon you're gonna do with that?

         Suddenly the mouse runs out again and EDDIE
         screams again and moves DEE *in front of him*.

EDDIE   Aagh! Oh my god, there it is! Shit they can move,
         can't they?

DEE   Yeah leave it.

         He screams again and moves again.

EDDIE   Aaagh!

DEE   Ow you got my foot!

                EDDIE *puts his cock away.*

                What are you doing?

EDDIE   It's alright.

DEE   We're gonna finish what we started.

EDDIE   It's alright.

DEE   I thought you were in to it.

EDDIE   I was. At the beginning but then –

DEE   What?

EDDIE   Never mind. The mouse, and then –

DEE   What?

EDDIE   You're just a little bit... drunk.

                DEE *is stung.*

DEE   Oh.
                Sorry.

EDDIE   Don't panic.
                You're still cute.

                Come here.

DEE   I can't you've hurt my ankle.

                EDDIE *helps her on to the bed, sits her on his knee and cuddles her. He rubs her ankle. DEE isn't sure whether she likes it or not, she thinks she probably does.*

EDDIE   You're a shambles.

DEE   Am I?

EDDIE   How many drinks did you have tonight?

DEE   Exactly enough.

EDDIE   Really?

DEE   Yes.

EDDIE   Come on.

DEE   What?

EDDIE   Look around you.

DEE   I told you not to do that.

EDDIE   It's not okay to live like this.

DEE   Like what?

EDDIE   Like… Don't you dread coming home?

DEE   Not how you pictured me is it?

EDDIE   Not really.

DEE   Unbecoming of a lady.

EDDIE   Don't do that.

DEE   Do what?

EDDIE   Make me sound like a dickhead.

DEE   I was joking.

EDDIE   Right.

DEE   So bossy.

EDDIE   No – I'm just –

DEE   It's hot.

           EDDIE *perks up*.

EDDIE   Really.

DEE   I knew you'd be like that from your profile.
           'You'll notice me for my imperious glare.'

EDDIE   Exactly.

DEE   Do it.

          EDDIE *does an imperious glare*.

          I feel tiny.

EDDIE   You are tiny.

          EDDIE *touches her nose*. DEE *pushes his face
          gently*.

2. Eddie 2. Vera 1

DEE *staggers into her room, giggling. It's dark.* VERA *staggers
after her. They are carrying wine*.

DEE   Let me see!

VERA   No!

          DEE *is trying to lift up* VERA*'s skirt*.

DEE   How can a pair of knickers cost forty-five quid?
          I need to see them!

VERA   You can have a little feel.

          VERA *lifts* DEE*'s hand up her skirt.* VERA *slaps*
          DEE*'s hand away*.

          Tha's 'nough!
          What would your boyfriend say?

DEE   Fuck him!

          VERA *roars with laughter*.

VERA   Can't see a thing.

DEE   Prioritise.

> DEE *is prioritising the wine.*

VERA   There's something about you.

DEE   How do you mean?

VERA   I don't know, baby, it's why I follow you round at
         the gym. I want to see into your eyes. There's
         something there.

DEE   What?

VERA   I don't know what it is. An edge.

DEE   I don't have an edge.

VERA   You would say that, wouldn't you?
         Where's the light?

> VERA *tries to switch the wall light on and off, it*
> *doesn't work.*

DEE   It doesn't work.

> VERA *turns on the torch light on her phone.*

VERA   Wow.
         Cool place.

DEE   Don't lie.

> *They both giggle uncontrollably as they pour some*
> *wine.* VERA *wanders into the bathroom.*

VERA   Babe.
         Why is there a pan in your shower?

> *They laugh even harder. The light comes on.*
>
> EDDIE *is sitting in* DEE's *bed, now awake.*
>
> VERA *sees him and stops laughing.* DEE *turns*
> *and sees him.*

EDDIE   Hi.

DEE   Oh.

EDDIE   Hi.

DEE   Hi darling. What's – this?

EDDIE   I thought I'd surprise you.

DEE   Oh my god.

EDDIE   But it looks like you've surprised me.

VERA   Hello.

DEE   This is Vera.

From the gym.

EDDIE   I'm Dee's / boyfriend.

VERA   I know.

Nice to meet you.

(*To* DEE.) Can I use your loo?

DEE   Yeah.

VERA *goes back into the bathroom.*

I am so sorry.

EDDIE   It's alright.

DEE   Me and Vera went to the pub after the gym.

EDDIE   I can see that.

DEE   We're not that drunk!

This is a nice surprise.

She kisses him.

EDDIE   I wanted to see you.

DEE   I'm seeing you tomorrow.

EDDIE   I know.

DEE   It's great. What a treat.

           VERA *flushes the toilet and comes out.*

VERA   So am I staying or am I going?

           DEE *looks at* EDDIE.

           EDDIE *laughs as he looks at her, like, 'What do
           you want me to do?'*

EDDIE   It's up to you darling.

           DEE *smiles awkwardly at* VERA.

DEE   Um – should we – do this another time maybe?

VERA   Okay.

           I mean, I was invited, sooo –

DEE   I know, I'm so – well actually, maybe we should
           all hang out, it's not late –

           EDDIE *laughs.*

EDDIE   What time is it?

DEE   Who knows! Wine?

EDDIE   Not for me.

VERA   Right.

           I forgot to wipe my arse so – I'll just go and
           do that.

           DEE *bursts out laughing.*

           VERA *goes back into the bathroom.*

           DEE *pulls out another bottle of wine.*

EDDIE   Wow. Funny lady.

DEE   Yeah.

EDDIE   Two bottles.

DEE   Yeah, do you want one too? I can pop down and
           get another one.

EDDIE   Not for me.

           EDDIE *laughs again.* DEE *laughs.*

DEE   What?

EDDIE   I'm just waiting for you to decide what you want
           to do kitten. Nobody can do anything until you've
           decided.

           EDDIE *lets out a little squeak. Pouts at her.*

           DEE *mimics it.*

           EDDIE *gets up and goes to her.*

           Getting all stressed. Come here.

           He pulls her on to his lap. He strokes her hair.

           Kitten.

DEE   (*In a tiny voice.*) I just – I – wanted to…

EDDIE   Hm?

DEE   (*Whispers.*) Vera's a new friend and I haven't
           made many friends except for you –

EDDIE   Well you've only been here a few weeks –

DEE   I know but she's fun and –

EDDIE   Alright. We'll fix it. Come here.

           EDDIE *holds her to him.*

           VERA *comes back out. He smiles at her, like,
           'Bye', but that she should be quiet.*

VERA   Bye then.

           DEE *sits up.*

DEE   Vera –

VERA   Next time.

DEE   I'm really sorry.

VERA   Don't you apologise.

           VERA *leaves.*

           DEE *turns to look at* EDDIE. *She notices some
           flowers in a pint glass.*

DEE   What's this?

EDDIE   They're for you.

DEE   Ahhh baby, they're lovely.

EDDIE   Not that there's any space for them.

DEE   I'll put them over here –

EDDIE   *Don't* move them. I just got them balanced.

DEE   You're so amazing, what did you do that for?

EDDIE   Because you deserve to wake up and see flowers.

           DEE *smiles.* EDDIE *beckons to her.*

           Now. Let me show you what I've been thinking of
           doing all day.

           She goes to him.

           EDDIE *starts to kiss her neck.*

DEE   I'm on my period.

EDDIE   Right you are.

            *He pulls his hands back like a shot, a look of
            nausea on his face.*

3. Miles 1

DEE *is standing.* MILES *lights up a cigarette.* DEE *hands him
a glass of wine. He takes the bottle and admires it.*

MILES   A Purple Angel. Well.

DEE   You came all this way. It was the least I could do.

MILES   'It was the least she could do, so that's what she
            did.'

            He sits.

            Do you ever think there's loads of people, and it's
            like almost everyone I know, whose main way of
            being 'good', is to patiently listen out for when
            other people say something wrong. And then call
            them on it. But never actually do anything.

DEE   Maybe.

            She fills up MILES*'s wine.*

MILES   I almost feel like they forfeit their right to
            comment, because they don't actually care.

DEE   Care about what?

MILES   The 'orthodox view'. Held by the self-appointed
            arbiters of right and wrong. Urban liberals in
            other words.

DEE   Is that me?

MILES   Oh god, probably – is the smoke blowing in?

DEE   No, it's okay.

           Then he looks up at her and cocks his head.

MILES   Don't you want to sit down?

           DEE *looks around for the chair. She moves the stuff off the chair and sits down, pulling in a little closer to him.* MILES *smokes and looks at her.* DEE *sips her wine.*

           Thirty-three years old. From Wales.

DEE   Spot-on.

MILES   Been in London – ?

DEE   Eight months. Maternity cover.

MILES   And you work in – marketing?

           DEE *nods.*

DEE   I'm a Planner.

MILES   (*Looking around him.*) That's ironic.

DEE   Don't you like my flat?

MILES   No.

           DEE *feigns shock.*

DEE   How rude.

           Tell me more about the school.

MILES   Why?

DEE   Because I know nothing about you. And I wanna keep you talking.

           And I can't believe they let you run your own school.

MILES   Jesus, they've been all over the press since 2010.

DEE   Have they?

MILES   (*Teasing*.) Well maybe not *your* press.

DEE   But you haven't got kids?

MILES   No.

DEE   So what so you and some mates are gonna club together and start your own curriculum?

MILES   The government, like tired parents, finally gave up and went, 'Oh for god's sake just do it yourselves then, if you're going to whinge.' And types everywhere have run with it.

DEE   Middle-class types.

MILES   Middle class is all of us. Middle class is sixty per cent of the country. People in the suburbs of Nottingham watching *X Factor*. We're talking about the educated urban bourgeoisie.

DEE   Upper-middle-class – elitists.

MILES   It's more of an intelligentsia.

DEE   The Tory Boys of the Future.

MILES   I didn't say that.

DEE   I got an idea for a school.

MILES   Oh yeah.

DEE   It's called the 'Give Everyone an Equal Chance, Not Just the Fucking Rich Kids' School.

MILES   Snappy.

DEE   What do you reck?

MILES   I 'reck' it's exactly the kind of comment I'd expect from someone like you.

DEE   Someone like me?

MILES   The kind of person who jumps to conclusions as
           soon as she thinks her little bell's being rung.

DEE   Her what?

           MILES *lights up another cigarette.*

MILES   You see yourself as a liberal. That's okay, that's
           very typical of people in your age and demographic.
           I do object to the absence of rigour though.

DEE   My absence?

MILES   Yes.
           There's an entire selection of attitudes that people
           like you assume you subscribe to because said
           attitudes belong in the liberal 'box', without
           having examined them for their individual merit.

DEE   Isn't that exactly what you're doing to me?

MILES   How?

DEE   Putting me in a box without having examined me.

MILES   Touché.
           Should I examine you more closely?

DEE   Is this part of the game? Me being dazzled by your
           genius?

           MILES *shakes his head gently.*

           When are we getting on with this?

MILES   Not yet.

           You're not ready yet.

4. Eddie 3

EDDIE *is cooking food.*

DEE   Why've you got so many saucepans?

EDDIE   I've bought cauliflower rice just for you.

DEE   Don't worry about it.

EDDIE   No, I've got some specially.

DEE   I'll just – I'll just have what you're having.

EDDIE   Why?

DEE   Because I'll get hungry.

EDDIE   But you said – okay.

DEE   What?

EDDIE   You said you were off carbs.

DEE   I haven't got time to impose constraints on
          my body.

EDDIE   Sure.

DEE   I'm cultivating my personality.

          EDDIE *doesn't really laugh.*

          I feel like you're disapproving a bit.

EDDIE   No.

          I just.
          I want you to be happy.

DEE   I've heard there are these pills, like this wonder-
          drug you can buy online that actually makes you
          want to do the things you should be doing, like
          staring your debts in the face, like it makes you
          overcome inertia, isn't that amazing?

EDDIE   And you want to pay money for this –

DEE   It's just a 'mood enhancer' like alcohol, or cigarettes...

EDDIE   So you're saying there's medicine for laziness now?

DEE   Not for 'laziness' – inertia.

EDDIE   If you want to be less lazy, kitten, try being a bit less lazy.

DEE   God.

EDDIE   What?

DEE   I won't buy any then.

EDDIE   Great.

        EDDIE *gets some wine out of his bag and puts it in a cupboard.*

DEE   What are you doing?

EDDIE   I'm gonna start leaving some wine here, so that we can have nice wine when we're round here. And not be relying on the selection of your friend on the corner.

DEE   Let's drink it now. Treat ourselves.

EDDIE   No.
        Tea.

        Over the next, DEE *turns the kettle on. She tries the lid of the coffee and pretends she can't open it. He puts his hand out for it and she gives it to him.*

DEE   What were they like, your exes?

EDDIE   What?

DEE   I mean, you know, Christina and that.

EDDIE   Tidier than you.

             DEE *laughs self-deprecatingly.* EDDIE *has found some mail on her table.*

             They opened their mail.

DEE   Oh yeah.

EDDIE   Shall I open it?

DEE   You don't want my mess.

EDDIE   Yes I do.

             EDDIE *opens the envelope whilst eyeballing* DEE. DEE *puts on a squirming face.*

DEE   No!

             She goes pathetically to grab the letter. EDDIE *whips it out of her way. He looks at the letter.*

EDDIE   Dear dear. Kitten hasn't paid her television licence.

DEE   Don't read that!

EDDIE   And she's gone over her overdraft limit – bad for your credit.

DEE   Give it here.

EDDIE   You're already in debt. Why haven't you opened these?

DEE   (*Girly.*) Because it's all overbearing, bureaucratic bullshit.

             Her phone buzzes. It's nearer him. He looks at it.

EDDIE   Hello Sam.

             DEE *snatches up the phone.*

             Again.

DEE   I thought I'd ask his advice about my loo if it gets any worse.

EDDIE   Oh he's a plumber is he?

DEE   He's not a plumber no, but he can turn his hand
to it.

EDDIE   I could turn my hand to it.

DEE   It's alright.

EDDIE   Shouldn't your landlord be doing that?

DEE   He won't get back to me.

EDDIE   Give me his number.

DEE   (*Hard.*) I've got it in control but thank you very
much for caring.

*EDDIE raises his eyebrows and withdraws from
her. He doesn't like being spoken to like that.*
DEE *adjusts.*

DEE *beams at him sweetly.*

Thank you for caring.

EDDIE   I do care.

DEE   I know you do. It's nice.

EDDIE   Tell Sam I can sort my own girlfriend's plumbing
out…

DEE   IF you know what I mean.

EDDIE   Hm?

EDDIE *doesn't get the joke.*

*She moves towards him and starts to kiss him. He
moves her away, sits her down.*

*He massages her shoulders. He gets a text. He
taps a response. She jokingly cranes her head to
see. He shifts the phone out of the way.*

DEE   What were they like? Bonnie and Christina. What
was Bonnie like?

EDDIE   How d'you mean?

DEE   Did you boss her around?

EDDIE   I don't boss you around, kitten. I train you.

DEE   And did Bonnie respond to training?

EDDIE   I – probably offered her advice from time to time.

DEE   And did she tell you to fuck off and stop trying to control her?

          They're sort of laughing.

EDDIE   No because she wouldn't have spoken like that.

DEE   What would she have said?

EDDIE   What, when I told her what I thought she should do?

DEE   Right, when you told her what you thought she should do.

EDDIE   She'd probably have said she appreciated that I cared about her.

DEE   Even if she was drunk?

EDDIE   She didn't drink that much.

DEE   Oh sure.

EDDIE   She'd have a glass of wine but she'd savour it. She was just a very – sweet person.

DEE   Stayed in during the week?

EDDIE   Mostly.

DEE   Same with Christina?

EDDIE   Sorry why are we talking about this?

DEE   Diminutive little attractive things that eat buckwheat and go to yoga.

EDDIE   You go to yoga, kitten.

DEE   I go yeah, I can't do it.

EDDIE   Well stop forking out for it and put the money
           towards moving out.

DEE   Tucked up by ten thirty with a herbal and a Kindle
           were they?

EDDIE   What?

DEE   Keeping an eye on the budget, leaving notes for
           housemates, packed lunch of leftovers, 'oh it's just
           leftovers', phoning her parents, wiping her fridge...

EDDIE   This is just babble now.

DEE   These women are liars.

EDDIE   Because they're not like you?

DEE   Ladies. Lovely feminine ladies. Leaving the party
           early, *'we're gonna go'*. Ladies who lunch ohhh it's
           so nice when it's just us *ladies*, spoiling ourselves
           with cocktails, clip-cloppy ladies' shoes, work those
           abs, steam those veggies. Ladies first. *LADIES*.

EDDIE   Right.
           Right.

DEE   What?

EDDIE   S'alright. I get it.

5. Vera 2

VERA *has a bag of MDMA.* DEE *has a plastic bag containing Haribo and cans of lager.*

VERA   I don't understand you baby, this was your idea.

DEE   I don't want to, Vera.

VERA   Come on babe, why not?

DEE   I'm just – happier without it.

VERA   You booked us the fucking taxi.

    VERA *hands her the bag.*

DEE   I don't want to, Vera!

    DEE *pulls a bottle of wine out.*

    Here, I've got this. It's one of Eddie's special Chilean ones.

VERA   Uhhh – he's not here again is he? Your boyfriend.

    VERA *checks in the wardrobe, under the bed.*

DEE   He's not here.

VERA   Creeping around your house in the dark like a – what they called? TARANTULA.

DEE   It's just us.

VERA   What if he lets himself in again?

DEE   He won't.
    I'm opening this.

VERA   *No* we gotta do both.

DEE   Why?

VERA   So it's equal. Why not?

DEE   I like to feel in control.

VERA   (*Pointing at the booze.*) What's this then?

DEE	C'mon I'm hammered already, don't make me take uppers when I'm already up.
VERA	Okay fine we won't do it.
DEE	What any of it?

VERA *shrugs and walks into the bathroom. We can hear her weeing.* DEE *sits on the bed. They shout to each other.*

VERA	You're the one with the *boyfriend*.
DEE	Don't worry about him.
VERA	This is sort of blocked you know?
DEE	I've stopped using it – you can pee in the shower.
VERA	What the fuck?!
DEE	I know, I'm sorry, I need to get it fixed.
VERA	How do you shit?
DEE	I do it in the gym sometimes.
VERA	I thought that was you! How do I flush it down now?
DEE	Use the shower.
VERA	Oh right.

The sound of the shower.

DEE	So you don't wanna do – anything now?
VERA	Not if you won't do MD with me. Tell me one reason baby why you're scared.

VERA *comes back in.*

DEE	It's not really me.
VERA	You're not in the Welsh Valleys any more girl.
DEE	You think they don't do MD in the Valleys that's all they do.

VERA	Take it from me, you're gonna want something.
DEE	Is what we're doing so weird to you?
VERA	What we might be doing, I haven't decided.

She burrows into the plastic bag on the bed and fishes out some Haribo, which she starts to eat.

Nah.

DEE	What?
VERA	Just everything. After the sudden like – 'no drugs' bombshell. Maybe I was in to it and maybe now I'm not.
DEE	Okay cool. You seemed pretty sure in the VIP room.
VERA	I really don't remember.
DEE	Really?
VERA	I have a little blank.
DEE	Oh would you like me to remind you?
VERA	Okay.
DEE	Would you like me to fill that little blank?
VERA	If you want.
DEE	Well the guys were all coming and going and I was sitting near where you were snogging Lance – who's so much less funny than he thinks he is by the way.
VERA	Is he?
DEE	So Lance got up and left and I was going to get my coat but you put your little finger on mine and you held me there until eventually everyone had gone?
VERA	No idea.

DEE   Just innocently waiting and no one suspected
       a thing.
       D'you remember that?

VERA   And then when we were finally alone, you turned
       to me, put two fingers under my chin and kissed
       me softly on the lips.

       VERA *smiles*.

       Lance is so fucking dry.

DEE   You *do* remember!

VERA   I was making you jealous, man. Cos I knew the
       idea was planted in your head.

DEE   Oh.

VERA   Like a seed, like a sexy little seed... that I put
       there.

       VERA *smiles at her. A moment*.

       That was when you kissed me.

DEE   No, you kissed me you fucker!

VERA   Well you were in to it.

DEE   Of course I'm in to it. I'm in to you.

       I always get a little shiver when you walk into
       the gym.

VERA   What?

DEE   You breeze.

VERA   (*Delighted*.) I what?

DEE   And you're funny.

VERA   I am fucking funny right?

DEE   Yeah.

VERA   What did you think about me when you met me?

DEE   In Spinning?

VERA   Yeah in Spinning.

DEE   I thought you were amazing.

VERA   But did you think I was approachable?

DEE   God no.

VERA   That's good.
           And did you think I was capable?

DEE   Sure.

           I always think of you as wearing these pale-pink
           vest tops.

VERA   Yeah pale pink's my colour. Good colour.

           VERA *nods, enjoying herself.*

           I wish my fucking mother could see me now.

DEE   She'd be proud.

VERA   No.
           She'd be wrong.

DEE   Well look at you now. Winning.

VERA   And I'm a really fucking good kisser.

DEE   You are.

VERA   Did you like the –

DEE   Yeah.

VERA   In the VIP room?

DEE   I really liked it.

VERA   Thank you that means a lot.

           So. Which bit did you want to do? Do you just
           want to kiss?

DEE   No.

VERA   You want to go further?

DEE   Yeah.

VERA   (*American high school.*) ALL THE WAY?!

DEE   I don't know, I want to experience it! Okay! Can't
           we just –

VERA   Alright then darling we will. We will.

           DEE *hesitates*.

           When you think about fucking a woman, which
           part of her body do you focus on?

DEE   Um…

VERA   Simple question.

DEE   Is it?

VERA   Yep.

DEE   I don't know…

VERA   Of course you know. Close your eyes.

DEE   I… think about her boobs a bit. I guess.

VERA   You like big ones? Like pillows? Or pointy little
           perky ones?

DEE   I like them both.

VERA   Sure but they have to be a certain shape don't
           they?

DEE   Hah. Yeah probably.

VERA   Yeah they can't be pointing downwards.

DEE   Um –

VERA   Yeah and I want no fat on her hips at all.

DEE   Okay.

VERA	Thick wavy hair and tiny little arms at the top.
DEE	Oh –
VERA	Fucking big tits and a waist like that.

She indicates a tiny waist that she can nearly get her hands around.

	And her pussy has to be really tight, you know?
DEE	Wow you. You think about... how tight her – ?
VERA	I know, hilarious isn't it? Teeny tiny shaven little angel hole.
DEE	But I'm not any of those things.
VERA	Neither am I baby, look at me. I wouldn't fuck myself.
DEE	So what –
VERA	I don't get it either.
	All I can say is my vagina is not my brain.
	And when I wank to these things I wank fast... and hard...
	And when I've cum I am disgusted.
	So.
	If that means you're not in to it, then I'll understand but I was just trying to be honest.

VERA moves to touch DEE and DEE recoils.

	What is it?
DEE	Vera – what you just said – that is horrible.
VERA	I know it's just the truth.
DEE	No but – where has that attitude –
VERA	Why do you care what I –

DEE   Because I don't have a teeny tiny angel hole!
           I've got a fucking *woodland mud cave*!

           VERA *starts laughing*. DEE *laughs with her.*

VERA   What's the mud?!

           You have a mud pussy?!

DEE   No, it's just not what you described.
           And it makes me feel like shit.

VERA   Let me see.

DEE   What?! No!

VERA   Let me see the mud cave.

DEE   There's absolutely no way you're seeing any part
           of me after that.

VERA   Just for a minute.

DEE   No.

VERA   Thirty seconds – and no touching.

DEE   I'm not interested.

VERA   Please.

DEE   No Vera.

VERA   Ten seconds. Ten seconds only. And then I promise
           I will leave you alone.

DEE   For god's sake! *Ten seconds then if it will shut
           you up!*

           VERA *wriggles into position.*

           Nothing else, no touching.

VERA   No touching.
            Are you ready?

            DEE *nods*.

            VERA *very gently reaches under* DEE*'s skirt,
            takes her knickers and pulls them off.*

            She gazes at DEE*'s vagina for ten seconds before*
            DEE *snaps her legs shut again.*

            VERA *smiles. Gently parts* DEE*'s legs again, and
            leans in to touch her.*

6. Miles 2

MILES *and* DEE *are in the same positions as before.*

DEE   So what sorts of things does a person 'like me'
            believe then?

MILES   All manner of woolliness, I'd say. Like
            immigration. You're part of that class who can't
            for the life of them see why immigration might be
            a problem because they live amongst immigrant
            communities and they love it. And of course they
            do because the only interaction with first-
            generation immigrants is to buy stuff from them.
            Eat their food. Have their apartment cleaned.
            Smile at their babies in queues. Maybe be treated
            by them at some of the better NHS outlets.

            DEE *wrinkles her nose uncomfortably.*

            Not quite the same as living on a housing list for
            four years and getting bumped down it every three
            months. Having kids without basic English
            suddenly join your daughter's class. Doing group
            revision on *Romeo and Juliet* with kids who can't
            follow.

DEE   Whoa.

MILES   Sorry?

DEE   Whoa just. Sorry.

MILES   What is it?

DEE   The way you're talking.

MILES   Go on.

DEE   I didn't think this was going to get all 'Farage'.

MILES   No. Because I sound racist right.

DEE   You sound like. A right-wing bigot.

MILES   Well I'm not right-wing or a bigot.

DEE   Immigrants prop up the economy. Lots are
          educated. They're an opportunity, not a burden.

MILES   *Guardian*.

DEE   No.

MILES   Oh come on.

DEE   What, that doesn't make it any less my opinion,
          does it?

MILES   I recognise that there's a generation below me of
          comfortable bourgeois kids. Who all studied the
          Holocaust in history. Who all know racism is evil.
          And who grew up believing that everyone's the
          same and borders probably shouldn't really exist.
          Who are frankly desperate to meet a racist so that
          they can really disagree with them. And as soon as
          someone talks about immigration their ears prick
          and they're like, 'I've got one! I've found a racist!
          In the flesh.'

          But you see all that happens with no borders is you
          have no government. No effective human systems,
          no welfare state, no public services, no civilisation
          and nothing that we've fought for since the
          Enlightenment. You can't let everyone in.

DEE   I didn't say you – wait. This is / bullshit.

MILES   Do you agree with what I'm saying?

DEE   No – no hang / on.

MILES   I'm hanging / on –

DEE   You're –

MILES   Don't start getting offended by me because you
        have some emotional feeling that you should be.

DEE   I'm not – I'm trying to –

        You're just gonna talk over me now.

MILES   No I'm not. Go on.

DEE   I'm not the one making the emotional argument.
        You're the one making the emotional argument.

MILES   Am I?

        DEE*'s drunk. She takes a deep breath.*

DEE   'The *foreigners* will take what's *rightfully* yours.'

        We only have those things by chance.

MILES   Really?

DEE   And secondly, I haven't finished. All this about
        'woolly and soft'

MILES   Is that a new point?

DEE   There's nothing wrong with being soft.
        Politics is about human beings.
        If we don't think about people, we are tyrants
        and fascists.

Why am I having a debate about immigration right now?

MILES   Because we're getting you ready.

Psychologically.

DEE   Why, is this war?

MILES   Sort of.

DEE   I know what you're doing to me. You're trying to make me feel weak.

MILES   Oh it's no fun for me if you're weak.

Stand up.

She does.

7. Vera 3

VERA *and* DEE *are in the same position as before.* VERA *is touching* DEE*'s vagina.*

DEE   This is the bit where if we were in a porn video, I'd start moaning, and tip my head back, like I was really in to it.

VERA   Do it anyway.

DEE *tips her head back and starts to make porn noises.* VERA *laughs, copies a bit.*

DEE   Oh yeah right there – auuuughhhh! Yeyeyeyeyeyeyeyeyeye / right there augh.

VERA   That's it the whiny pain sound.

They laugh.

Okay, I'm going in.

DEE   Oh that's it for the foreplay is it?

VERA   I'll do some more in a bit. I just want to –

VERA's expression changes as she inserts her fingers into DEE's vagina.

Ohhoohohooo Jesus that is – there that is a feeling like… wowww.

DEE   Uh-huh?

VERA   Oh man, you have got to try this, I mean there's something fucking holy about it.

DEE   Really?

VERA   Yeah it's the fucking tits. Does it feel good?

DEE   Obviously.

VERA   Okay I'm sliding it now.

DEE   I know…

VERA   Every woman should do this. Every woman needs to know what someone else's I mean, fuck! I am experiencing my own vagina objectively. Thank you for this privilege.

DEE   You really don't have to thank me.

VERA   It's like… suddenly loads of things make sense. I feel deeply honoured.

I wanna do it perfect – Tell me what to do.

DEE   Maybe let's be quiet for a bit?

VERA   Sure sure.

VERA is twisting her arm around.

I'm touching the G-spot?

DEE   Yeah I think so.

VERA   Does it make you want to piss?

DEE	Sort of yeah. Ow – maybe –
VERA	Lighter, yeah. Shall I do this and, that?
DEE	Can you – can you keep that up?
VERA	Of course.
DEE	Sure?
VERA	Not forever – but –

DEE *stops* VERA.

DEE	It's hurting your hand.
VERA	So?
DEE	I can't concentrate if I think it's hurting your hand.
VERA	Why do you care?
DEE	Because it puts me off.
VERA	I'm gonna keep going.
DEE	Can you stop asking me what you should do then?
VERA	Why?
DEE	Just do whatever you do to yourself.
VERA	What do you do to yourself?
DEE	I don't know.

VERA *stops and sits back.*

VERA	Why don't you want to tell me?
DEE	Do what you wish someone would do to you.
VERA	There isn't anything I wish – I want something, they do it.
DEE	What you just say, 'stroke my – do this'.
VERA	Sure.

VERA *starts again.*

DEE	No you don't. Ahhhhh.
VERA	Yes I do. Don't you?
DEE	No.
VERA	It makes you feel dirty?
DEE	No…
VERA	What would you want a man to do?
DEE	Stop talking about men. Ahhhhh.

DEE *is getting in to it.*

VERA	Yeah it's good?
DEE	Yeah it's good.
VERA	I'm gonna make you cum?
DEE	Yeah probably.
VERA	Cos I'll be able to tell if you're faking cos you know, I'm a woman.
DEE	Oh well probably not then.
VERA	(*Suddenly incensed.*) You're fucking kidding me?

VERA *stops.*

DEE	I'm sorry.
VERA	You were gonna fake for me?! One of your own?!
DEE	Okay –
VERA	I cannot believe this shit!
DEE	Vera –
VERA	No fuck you, girls don't fake with another girl, that's the fucking rule.
DEE	Alright.
VERA	What the fuck d'you think feminism is for?

DEE   Not that.

VERA   Yes, the sisterhood man!

DEE   I've said I'm sorry!

           Can we carry on?

VERA   I need a piss.

           VERA *goes into the bathroom and pees into the bottom of the shower.*

           DEE *is overcome with emotion. She cries.*

           VERA *comes back in and sees her.*

           DEE *tries to cover her emotion, but* VERA *has noticed.*

           You weren't sposed to get upset.

DEE   No it's just – it wasn't – I just.

VERA   I was just saying don't lie to me.

DEE   I know, I'm not getting upset about that.

VERA   Did I hurt you?

DEE   No.
           Just gimme a hug please.

8. Eddie 4

DEE *is holding her head on the bed. She has just confessed to*
EDDIE *that she slept with* VERA *and is feeling guilty.*

EDDIE   What did you do?

DEE   We kissed a lot. Touched each other.

EDDIE   Did you kiss below the neck?

DEE   Yes.
          A lot.

EDDIE   *South?*

DEE   All of that.

EDDIE   With all the –

DEE   Everything you can imagine.

          I'm so sorry.

EDDIE   When was it?

DEE   Saturday.

EDDIE   The night you were 'just going for a beer with the
          gym lot and it wasn't worth me coming'?

DEE   Yeah.

EDDIE   Was Lance there?

DEE   Yeah.

EDDIE   Was he coming on to you again?

DEE   What? No.

EDDIE   See you don't notice these things.

DEE   I do – I –

EDDIE   You don't, kitten.

DEE   Why are we talking about Lance?

EDDIE   What?

DEE   I've just told you I got off with Vera.

EDDIE   Oh.

DEE   Is that all you've got to say?

We were hammered.
I know that's not an excuse.

I feel absolutely –

EDDIE   Next time, invite me.

DEE   To the drinks?

EDDIE   No, I mean. I might like to watch.

DEE   What?

EDDIE   Next time, invite me, I might like to watch.

DEE   Are you joking?

EDDIE   What?

DEE   Don't you care what I do?

EDDIE   Of course I care

DEE   But only if it's with a bloke.

EDDIE *shrugs*.

EDDIE *laughs*. DEE *doesn't*.

EDDIE   What is this?

DEE   I'm trying to –

EDDIE   I've just forgiven you.

DEE   Was there anything to forgive?

EDDIE   That's up to me isn't it?

DEE   Apparently you found it sexy.

             EDDIE *laughs. Shakes his head.*

EDDIE   Okay. Just – okay.

DEE   What?

EDDIE   You. You're something.

DEE   Why?

EDDIE   Ingratitude.

DEE   I'm ungrateful now?

EDDIE   I think so.

DEE   What am I ungrateful for?

EDDIE   If you have to ask –

DEE   For all that you do for me?

EDDIE   Yes.

DEE   For putting up with me?

EDDIE   Yes.

DEE   My deviant sex drive?

EDDIE   What is your problem tonight?

DEE   Have I not been fucking clear?

EDDIE   Not really.

DEE   Well I can *explain* it to you, my love, but I cannot *understand* it for you.

             EDDIE *glares at her.* DEE *turns to look at him square-on, instinctively readying herself for what's to come.*

EDDIE   You should hear yourself sometimes, kitten, seriously, you should hear yourself go. Newsflash. You are not as clever as you think you are. There are women out there who are doing better than you at being a woman. Who enjoy being a woman. And who have their fucking shit together. I can see you very clearly and it's not a particularly pretty picture if I'm honest. You've got a huge student loan, maxed-out credit cards, you're convinced this maternity cover will go permanent but your hangovers tell a different story and the bulk of your wages go to Topshop. You're messy, you're actually kind of dirty. This is where you live. There's a reason a lot of men don't subscribe to feminism, and it's cos it stinks of excuses. Clean yourself up, earn some respect and maybe then you'll get the equality you self-righteously claim to deserve.

There.

DEE *is shaken with anger.*

EDDIE *is getting his stuff.*

DEE   You've been planning that.

EDDIE   Oh fuck off.

DEE   Who said anything about feminism anyway?

EDDIE *shakes his head at her. He laughs. He packs his stuff up and leaves.*

9. Vera 4

VERA *is in her coat, and has just arrived with a bottle of wine.*
She's looking in the bathroom.

VERA	I can't believe your toilet is still blocked.
DEE	I know.
VERA	Can't you get a plumber in?
DEE	I can – I need to contact Sam about it.
VERA	Sam?
DEE	My ex.
VERA	I know who he is. I thought he was a carpet-fitter.
DEE	Yes. The carpet-fitter I used to love.
VERA	So why are you asking him questions about your toilet if he's a carpet-fitter? Is it because you still love the carpet-fitter?
DEE	No...

VERA *comes out of the bathroom.*

VERA	What do you want tonight? Do you want a friend or a fuck?
DEE	Oh – uhhhh...

VERA *starts to pour the wine.*

VERA	I'm glad you texted, really. It's good to see you. Either way I don't mind, I just like to know.
DEE	Um... Friend.
VERA	Friend, alright.

VERA *hands* DEE *a glass of wine.*

VERA *sits on the bed.*

Tell me about your ex.

DEE   I don't want to talk about Eddie.

VERA   Not Eddie. Sam.

DEE   Oh. Okay.

VERA   Are you still in touch?

DEE   Oh god yeah. He's with some weird ten-year-old junior sales assistant at the moment.

VERA   I was about to ask if you were over it.

DEE   Hah.

VERA   Totally over it

DEE   Totally over it.

           I stalk her online.

VERA   She probably stalks you worse.

DEE   Mm.

VERA   Why d'you break up?

DEE   (*Shrugs.*) Kids.

VERA   You want them.

DEE   Apparently I do.

           Imagine it though.

           DEE *holds her hands in a round shape at her stomach and stares at it.*

           Ba BOOM, ba BOOM, ba BOOM, ba BOOM.

VERA   I know.

           Do you think he'll change his mind?

           DEE *shrugs.*

DEE   Who's your person?

VERA   Ugh, wouldn't go back to any of them.

DEE   Why not?

VERA   You've got to look forwards. Got to go through it.
           Trudge, trudge, trudge.

           Like the *Bear Hunt*.

DEE   The what?

VERA   The *Bear Hunt* – I would do it when I was
           au-pairing.

           She chants the refrain from We're Going on a
           Bear Hunt, *makes a noise of swishing through the
           forest.*

           S'good.

DEE   If the perfect guy came along now, I think I'd
           punch him.

           VERA *laughs.*

VERA   Why?

           DEE *goes into the bathroom.*

DEE   First of all, where have you been? Second of all,
           I don't want you any more, I've got shit to do.
           Thirdly, you don't know me, you'll never know
           me. I'm thirty-three. I've already formed my
           personality.

VERA   Why does he need to know you?

           DEE *cranks the chain. It sounds broken.*

           I just want someone to go to the movies with.

DEE   Dream big.

           DEE *comes out of the bathroom and looks at*
           VERA. *They smile at each other.*

VERA   What?

DEE   You look perfect lying there.

           DEE *takes a picture with her phone.*

VERA	What was that?

DEE giggles.

DEE	Actually that's not a particularly flattering photo.

She shows VERA. VERA *yelps and tries to grab the phone.*

VERA	Give that here.

DEE	Just a little keepsake, you look cute.

VERA	Delete it.

DEE	I won't show anybody.

VERA	I'm not having people see that.

DEE	Hey you can trust me.

VERA	I don't trust anybody, let me delete it.

VERA *deletes the photo and gives it back.*

DEE	Course that's not the only place it's stored on my phone.

VERA	What? Give it back.

DEE *is backing to the other side of the room. She presses buttons on her phone.*

DEE	This'll look great on Instagram.

VERA	Dee.

DEE	What?

VERA	Dee.

DEE	Coupla clicks.

VERA	You fucking. Dare.

DEE	The rudeness!

She taps the phone. She smiles at the image. Suddenly VERA *flips.*

VERA	FUCK YOU YOU FUCKING PIG-FACED FUCKING CUNT BITCH, GIMME YOUR FUCKING PHONE! GIMME YOUR PHONE YOU LITTLE PRICK.

VERA *wrestles* DEE *to the ground and wrests the phone off her.*

Gimme the password!
AAAAHAHHGHGHHHGHH!

VERA *waves the phone in the air.*

WHAT'S THE FUCKING PASSWORD OR
I WILL FUCKING KILL YOU.

DEE	I didn't upload – I didn't upload anything, I was joking.
VERA	You expect me to believe that?
DEE	I was joking, give me the phone back and I'll show you.
VERA	You think I'm gonna give it to you now?
DEE	Wait!
VERA	I'll drop it out the fucking window.

VERA *holds it out the window.*

DEE	No! Vera I promise you I was joking, I wouldn't do that in a million years.
VERA	You better be fucking telling the truth.
DEE	I am telling the truth, please believe me, please.

DEE *is holding her hand out for her phone.*

VERA *brings her arm in, drops the phone, wanders over to the bed and crumples in a ball.* DEE *picks it up and rubs her arm.*

Fucking *hell* Vera.

VERA *stifles a sob*.

What was that about?

I was joking mate.

VERA   Why would you joke about something like that?

DEE   You work in PR. Take a day off.

Who cares if people see you without a fucking filter.

VERA   You don't care, that's up to you. But you will never be…

VERA *gestures – herself.*

DEE   What?

VERA   You will laugh at me because you don't get it.

DEE   Tell me. I will never be what?

VERA *laughingly more clearly gestures herself looking perfect and proud.*

Oh.

Yeah okay I get that.

10. Paddy 1

PADDY *is fiddling with a pink box of condoms.*

PADDY   He looked like I'd slapped him. Shook his head.
Well I wasn't having that. I stood my ground, said,
'I can see you've got some, there in the cabinet
behind you. A goodly selection of spermicidal
options and an ultra-thin variety for better
sensation.

But I wouldn't be half a man if I didn't opt for the
brand that maximised her pleasure, so I'll take the
ribbed ones please. Pink box.' He reaches into the
dusty little glass cabinet, pulls out the johnnies
and virtually chucks 'em at me. Then he has to
pick 'em up again with bony fingers to check the
price on them. He was shaking by the end of it.

DEE   (*Pointing out of the window.*) THAT is an old man.

PADDY   Well THAT shouldn't be left in charge of the shop
then, should it if THAT can't serve the customers.

DEE   He's lived a whole life, doesn't need your shit.

PADDY   I'm so sorry.

DEE   You should be.

PADDY   Getting so turned on by how sorry I am.

DEE   Kiss that.

DEE *offers him her foot, flirtatiously.*

PADDY   Now we're both turning me on. We can't both turn
me on.

DEE   I'm waiting…

PADDY *pinches her toe. She squeals. He looks
around.*

PADDY   Look at your place.

DEE   Don't be mean.

PADDY   No I just never thought you'd live somewhere like this.

DEE   Well when I get a permanent job after the maternity leave.

PADDY   You mean 'if'.

DEE   I'm working my tits off.

PADDY   Yes you are.

DEE   What the fuck would you know, intern?

PADDY   Nothing necessarily.

DEE   If you claim for a second that you don't still live with your parents I will die of shock.

PADDY   I do.

DEE   HAah!

PADDY   I'm still a teenager.

DEE   I know.

PADDY   You like it.

DEE   I'm mortified.

PADDY   Planned it from ages ago.

DEE   Me?

          She scoffs at the very idea. PADDY *does an impression of her 'scoffing'.*

PADDY   Pitching your tone with me, careful not to patronise, saving up eye contact and then BANG! (*Demonstrates her intense gaze.*) Paralysing glare.

          Sauntering to your desk with your stockings out.

DEE   I wore them once.

PADDY   Flirty little negs.

DEE   Negs?

PADDY   'That's a very strange choice of shirt, Paddy.'

DEE   It was a very strange choice of shirt.

PADDY   DON'T pretend you don't know what negging is, you minx.

DEE   Funny little thing, aren't you?

PADDY   THERE YOU GO AGAIN.

DEE   Shh.

PADDY   (*Quieter.*) My mates and I were styling out that pick-up nonsense in fucking prep school.

DEE   Oh god, you're posh.

PADDY   Of course I'm posh.

DEE   You don't sound posh.

PADDY   You don't sound desperate.

           She laughs.

           Am I ruined for you now?

DEE   Little bit.

PADDY   Thought I was your bit of dirty rude boi? Yagetme?

DEE   Yes I did.

PADDY   I know you did you perve. But I wouldn't be here right now if I was state educated.

DEE   Why not?

PADDY   Cos state schoolkids don't intern at Wilder and Sucks. They ain't got the contacts, the looks, or the chat.

DEE   The looks?

PADDY   Rich father – beautiful mother. 'Twas ever thus.
         Plus state schoolkids want paying.

DEE   Know any, do you?

PADDY   More importantly they'd never make a play for
         a woman like you. Takes a particular brand of
         confidence.

DEE   So self-aware.

PADDY   Adorable isn't it?

DEE   I bagged you actually.

PADDY   Is exactly what you were supposed to think.

         *They smile at each other. The moment holds. He's
         standing close to her, pleased with himself. He puts
         his arms round her. He holds her face. He starts to
         kiss her. She responds. He pulls off her top. He
         looks down at her bra. It's not a very sexy one.*

         Oooh.

DEE   What?

         He flicks her bra.

PADDY   Hm.

         DEE *covers herself.*

DEE   I wasn't – I didn't think it was going to happen
         tonight I –

PADDY   Don't panic. Just. Thought you were in to all that.

DEE   What?

PADDY   Nice stuff. The stockings.

DEE   I have some lacy stuff and some normal stuff.

PADDY   And this is your normal stuff is it?

DEE   Paddy.

PADDY   What?

DEE   There's certain – things – you learn as you get
          a bit older.

PADDY   Right.

DEE   I don't want to be patronising.

PADDY   Sure.

DEE   Just that the impression you get of a woman
          depends entirely on what we choose to hide
          from you.

PADDY   Makes sense.

DEE   Some men find that honesty really sexy.

PADDY   Yeah I know that, it's just –

DEE   What?

PADDY   I don't want to offend you.

DEE   Say it.

PADDY   Just.
          Some girls are a bit scuzz.

DEE   Is that so?

PADDY   Little bit.

DEE   And am I a scuzz girl now, because of my bra not
          being, what, lacy enough for you?

PADDY   Would we say you were a girl?

DEE   Answer the question.

PADDY   Do you think I'm talking about muff stuff?

DEE   Are you talking about 'muff stuff'?

PADDY   No. Just – you expect us to put our full face in
          there.

DEE	Hang on.
PADDY	It'd be nice if –
DEE	Hang on you little shit, I don't expect fucking anything.
PADDY	Alright!
DEE	And most of the time I don't get it anyway so don't be putting it on me or any extension of me / which constitutes –
PADDY	Alright!
	I'm just talking from my experience.
DEE	Have you had much?
PADDY	Maybe.
DEE	Alright then, how many girls have you had sex with?
PADDY	That's a personal question.
DEE	That many is it?
PADDY	More than you probably.
DEE	More than me?
PADDY	I've lost count.
DEE	Don't be coy.
PADDY	It happens a lot.
DEE	Every day?
PADDY	No.
	Four times a week maybe on average.
DEE	Liar!
PADDY	More some weeks than others.

DEE   I know what fucking 'average' means you liar!

PADDY   You don't have to believe me.

DEE   You saying you've slept with hundreds of women?

PADDY   Well I started when I was thirteen so.

           (*Laughs*.) Honestly it's a lot. Not sure how many
           any more. I don't know why I'm telling you this.

DEE   Which girls?

PADDY   Just. Girls. This is a city I have a phone. All kinds
           of anything. And they're bang up for it. Wouldn't
           be there if they weren't.

DEE   Where?

PADDY   They're called dating apps, Delilah.
           Now.
           (*Very RP.*) Where the devil were we?

           *He grabs her in a clinch. He puts her hand on his
           cock.*

DEE   Oh god it's massive.

PADDY   I know it's so embarrassing.

DEE   I know so many people who deserve it more
           than you.

PADDY   Don't tell anyone.
           (*Whispers*.) Tell everyone.

DEE   Bet this goes down well with the Tinder girls.

PADDY   So you do know about Tinder then?

DEE   A bit.

PADDY   A bit?

DEE   What happened to the days when a boy threw
           pebbles at your window?

PADDY   Old-fashioned romance?

DEE   Yeah.

PADDY   So your profile's not – you 'posing all cray-cray
           next to a hot-dog sign'?!

           He does the pose. DEE *cringes.*

DEE   Oh no.

PADDY   'Can't believe you're so muddy at the festival!'

DEE   Fuck off.

PADDY   'Serious. Selfie. With sunglasses.'

           Bikini and shorts.

DEE   Loads of girls have one of those.

PADDY   You don't have to tell me.

DEE   And those girls don't just want sex.

PADDY   Are you saying they enjoy it less than men?

DEE   No. You can't get me with that.

PADDY   Are you hoping we're gonna get married?

DEE   You're only five.

PADDY   So what are you saying?

DEE   Women use sex to get love, sometimes.

PADDY   In your generation, maybe.

DEE   Oh god are we two generations?

PADDY   Yep.

DEE   Oh god.

PADDY   We've come a long way, beautiful. The game's
         changed. The girls are up for it. Women of your
         generation are like…

         Beat. She smiles, daring him. He smiles back.

DEE   Go on.

PADDY   Last of a dying breed?

         He does an energetic impression of a dinosaur.

         DEE *shudders.*

DEE   (*To distract herself from that reality.*) Enough.
         Kiss me. Kiss my neck and try and pretend
         you're thirty.

PADDY   If I was thirty I wouldn't be here.

DEE   Why not?

PADDY   I'd be in New York.

DEE   Wow.

         DEE *stops.*

         PADDY *grabs her and puts her up against
         something. She can't help liking it. Hand on
         her neck. He slowly, assuredly, softly speaks
         into her ear.*

PADDY   Don't you worry your pretty, empowered
         independent
         little head
         about what's going to happen next.
         I'm going to take care of everything.

         He is kissing her neck. She's responding.

         But she breaks out.

DEE   Actually. No.
         You're going home.

PADDY   Are you serious?

DEE *waits. Hesitates.*

(*Whiny.*) Dee. I really want to.
Every day at work I think about you.
I'm only wanking to blonde porn stars because
of you.
The brunettes don't get a look-in.

DEE   Aww.

PADDY   I've got it bad.

DEE   It's not gonna happen.

PADDY   We can play long-term boyfriends and girlfriends
           if it gets you going.

DEE   I don't want to.

PADDY   I'm really looking forward to seeing your parents
           next weekend

           Electricity passes through DEE*'s body.*

DEE   Stop it.

PADDY   We'll have to put a wash on before Monday.

DEE   You're such a weirdo.

           Do it again.

PADDY   Let's set up a budget so we can save to buy a house.

DEE   Oh god yeah.

PADDY   In a good catchment area.

           For the schools.

DEE   Auughhh!

11. Miles 3

DEE *and* MILES *as before. She has her back to him.*

MILES   I like this dress.
          It flatters you.

DEE   Thank you.

MILES   Where did you grow up?

DEE   Swansea born and bred.

          Look. I don't mind getting into big debates like
          this but I don't want to be made to feel stupid.
          Like don't tell me who I am or what I think,
          alright? Because you might not be right about that.

MILES   Brothers and sisters?

DEE   No.

MILES   Shoes off.

          She takes her shoes off.

DEE   You've got a massive brain. But you can't tell me
          what I think, alright? Human beings are not types.
          Let people surprise you, Miles.

          People surprise me all the time.

MILES   Do I surprise you?

DEE   Yes.

MILES   Why?

DEE   Because you – don't add up.

MILES   Really?

DEE   Don't you feel marginalised by all – this that
          you're into?

MILES   I suppose I see it as two sides of the same penny.

DEE   I don't believe you.

MILES   Alright brat.
             I think you're ready.

12. Paddy 2

DEE *is in bed.* PADDY *is pulling on his clothes. He goes to kiss her on the cheek.*

DEE   You have to pee in the shower.

PADDY   Well actually I was going to erm –

DEE   You don't have to go.

             PADDY *smiles at her as he gets dressed.*

             DEE *pulls on a dressing gown.*

PADDY   I couldn't sleep for the snoring.

             DEE *tries to swallow her embarrassment.*

             Don't worry, I won't tell anyone.

DEE   I have these really fine delicate, nasal tissues
             actually –

PADDY   I meant about the sex. I'd look like a bit of a dick
             if I went telling everyone at work you snored like
             a banshee.

DEE   Banshees wail.

PADDY   That's what it sounded like.

He does a mean impression of her, climbing on to the bed, snoring/wailing right into her ear.

DEE *is laughing along but something in her snaps.*

DEE   Okay – just – fuck off mate, if you're gonna go.

PADDY   *You* can tell anyone you want about the sex. I'm sure they'd love to hear about *this*.

DEE   (*Laughing.*) I'm sure they would.

PADDY   What?

DEE   Go on, off you go. I'm glad you got your tiny little rocks off.

PADDY   (*Protesting.*) Eh!

Happy to take any feedback.

I'm serious.

DEE   Three stars.

PADDY   Out of what?

You sounded pretty happy.

DEE   Yes well.

PADDY   Well what? You made coming noises.

           They both sort of laugh.

           Are you being sarcastic?

DEE   Reassessing your week?

PADDY   You didn't say.

DEE   You didn't ask.

PADDY   What am I supposed to ask?
           'Did you get what you wanted?' Like I'm Father
           fucking Christmas.

DEE   Ask at the time.

EDDIE   I know but –

DEE   Rule of thumb, we notice everything.

PADDY   I noticed the hair on your lower back.

DEE   Deny that you hate giving oral sex.

PADDY   It's difficult.

DEE   Okay. Go on…

PADDY   You know what, / I don't care –

DEE   Have you ever even thought about what it feels
           like to sleep with you?

PADDY   No.

DEE   Asked anyone?

PADDY   No.

DEE   Read any books?

PADDY   (*Laughing*.) No.

           She picks up a book and throws it at him.

           Well I'd better fucking leave you to finish yourself
           off then.

           PADDY *fiddles with his phone*.

           DEE *sighs*.

DEE   I didn't mean it.

PADDY   It's alright. I've seen it before.
           Women of your age staring into the abyss…

DEE   Careful Paddy.

PADDY   I thought you'd be grateful.

DEE   Get the FUCK OUT OF HERE.

           *She throws another book at him. He leaps out of
           the way and exits.* DEE *sits in her bed. Shocked.
           Sad. Then not sure what to do.*

           *After a moment, there is a gentle knock on the
           door.*

           She gets up and opens it. It's PADDY.

PADDY   Sorry.

DEE   About what?

PADDY   Mean stuff.

DEE   Oh. Well.

I threw a sex book at a teenager.

PADDY   My battery's run out.

DEE   I'll book you an Uber.

PADDY   No, it's – if I can borrow your phone, I'll just –
call my mum. She'll –

DEE   It's two o'clock in the morning!

PADDY   She doesn't mind.

DEE *hands him her phone.*

Then she puts her hand on the bag of drugs
VERA *left.*

DEE *looks at him.*

DEE   You wanna get high?

13. Miles 4

DEE *and* MILES. *Same as before.*

DEE   Okay. Oh god.

MILES   Nervous?

DEE   Yes.
            Where shall I –

            MILES *puts out his cigarette and sits on the edge
            of the bed.*

MILES   Stand up.

            She does.

            Why are you here Dee?

DEE   Well I live here, so –

            DEE *looks like she's going to laugh.* MILES *looks
            amused.*

MILES   Figuratively not literally.

DEE   Why am I in this situation?

MILES   Yes.

DEE   Would you call yourself a situation?

MILES   Yes.

DEE   What do you want me to say / *'because I've been
            a bad girl'*?

MILES   The truth.

DEE   The truth is I was curious.

MILES   About what?

DEE   About you.

MILES   About men like me.

DEE   Yes, men like you. If you exist. What you do.
            What it means…

MILES   I don't think that's the whole truth.

DEE   Does it matter?

MILES   This is a mutual arrangement.

DEE   I know.

MILES   So give me something too.
            Why are you here?

14. Paddy 3

PADDY *and* DEE *are taking MDMA. There's music playing.*

They are looking at some dresses on the bed/hung up.

PADDY *runs his hands along the dresses for a second.*
Touches one.

DEE   What about the blue one? Bit more conservative.

PADDY   I like the red.

DEE   Blue one.

PADDY   Red one.

            Okay.

            DEE *hands him some shoes.*

DEE   I think these'll work.

PADDY   You joking?

DEE   No. It's going to be a breathtaking insight.

PADDY	Into you?
DEE	Into women.
PADDY	Cos of a dress?
DEE	Cos of what I'm gonna do to you in a dress.
PADDY	Remember your future career depends on me.
DEE	It's not a trick.
PADDY	Now am I wearing it with my boxers or are you going to insist I wear some tiny lacy scrap of gossamer to go underneath?
DEE	Wait right there.

DEE goes rummaging in her overstuffed underwear drawer.

Oh my god I've got hold-ups if you want?

PADDY	(*Spinning round.*) It's what I'm saying, wear them to work.

She hands him the stockings.

DEE	You're loving this, are you loving –

PADDY glares at her. DEE drops her smile.

Thank you. So much. This is going to blow your mind.

PADDY nods. He grabs some underwear.

Wait.

Over the next, PADDY gets dressed in DEE's dress and DEE puts on PADDY's shirt with a pair of her own jeans. She applies make-up to his face.

PADDY	Where did this dress come from then?
DEE	I wore it in September.
PADDY	Beautiful month.

DEE   For my interview for the maternity cover. It was
            boiling hot and I'd just got off the train and I was
            booked to look round some studio flats in 'South
            Kensington'.

PADDY   Aww… South Kensington.

DEE   South Kensin/gton.

PADDY   South Kensington.

DEE   I know, I was proper fresh off the boat. Didn't
            know anyone. Had to fight my way through the
            Tube at Paddington.

PADDY   Paddington.

DEE   But I was so happy that I was smiling at everyone.
            Some guy was smiling at me on the platform, and
            he was alright looking, so I looked him right in the
            eye and beamed at him.

PADDY   Oh no.

DEE   He got straight on the same carriage, sat next to
            me, started asking all these questions. He was fun,
            said he had this feeling that he just had to find out
            who I was, take me for a cocktail.

PADDY   Cocktail…

DEE   But as more people came on, I could feel them
            staring. Some woman gave me a look and shook
            her head. That's when I noticed he was twisting
            this old Sainsbury's bag in his hands while he
            talked. In the end, I handed him a couple of quid.
            I said, '*Bye*', kind of like that. He looked a bit
            shocked, but he left.

            I always felt bad about that.

PADDY   Two quid is plenty.

DEE   No. I mean I humiliated him.

PADDY   Cocktail. Cocktail.

When DEE *has finished,* PADDY *stands. He looks
beautiful. The tension is electric.* DEE *walks to
a chair and sits down and watches him.*

DEE   Hello.

DEE *smiles slowly.*

Turn around.

PADDY *turns around slowly. He's nervous but
styling it out.*

DEE *beckons him.*

*She puts on some music. They kiss and then dance
all around the space.*

*She as the man, he as the woman. She dips him
and spins him round.*

She sits down and looks at him.

PADDY   Shall I –

DEE   Shuttup.

He walks forward and DEE *touches his legs,
traces a finger up the stockings slowly up to
his arse.*

PADDY *does some showing-off dancing.*

She seems unmoved.

Do you know what, I think we should stop this.

PADDY   Why?

DEE   You're too high
               It's not really turning me on.

PADDY   (*Playful.*) Oohh I get it – swipe swipe Tinder
               Tinder swipe swipe – you've moved on already –
               I'm shapes to you – just a series of pretty skirts…

DEE   No no I'm sorry I'm just –

PADDY   Over me already?!

DEE   It's depressing me.

PADDY   Charming.

DEE   Those are my dresses. I actually wear them.
           I actually do that. I am that.

           Fuck.

           PADDY *is standing. His skirt still swishing.*
           He doesn't know what to do.

PADDY   I think they are lovely.

DEE   Of course you do.

           I'm going to book you that cab. Where do you live?

PADDY   South Kensington.

15. Sam 1

DEE *is tidying while she talks to* SAM, *who is in the bathroom with his back to us, wearing a boiler suit.*

DEE   Because I could rustle up a bowl of cereal?

SAM   I'm fine.

DEE   Piece of toast?

SAM   No.

DEE   Or I do a really quick, houmous, avocado with ham, tomato and spinach burrito.

SAM   Woman!

DEE   Alright alright, you've eaten.

        Hold on. Isn't it –

SAM   What?

DEE   Isn't it, isn't it Saturday?

SAM   Of course it's Saturday.

DEE   Are you injured?

SAM   No, I'm fine.

DEE   You're missing your football game. Are you missing your football game for me?

SAM   Well I'm not there am I?

DEE   I can't believe you're missing your football game to do. This.

SAM   Yes. It was more important to me. Your poo problem.

        SAM *comes out of the bathroom.*

        Not really, they dropped me.

        From the team.

DEE   Oh baby.

Why's that?

SAM   Because there are better players. And I don't
practise enough. I'm getting old.

DEE   The bastards.

SAM   It's a very unsentimental sport.

Your hair's grown.

DEE   Oh it's – erm.

It's a clip-in.

SAM   Serious?

She nods, shyly and touches it.

DEE   (*Decisive.*) Right!

DEE *dances to a corner of the room with glasses
and a bottle of wine.*

SAM   Not for me.

She opens the screw top.

DEE   Whoops!

SAM   It's two o'clock.

DEE   And I've accidentally opened an exquisitely
expensive bottle of wine...

SAM   Not a Blossom Hill Shiraz?

DEE   Chilean Cabernet 2008.

SAM   And that's good?

DEE   It will be. Eddie gave it to me.

She starts pouring.

Or at least he has now.

       SAM takes a glass.

SAM   How long were you with him?

DEE   Five fucking months mate.

SAM   Tinder?

DEE   Yep.

SAM   Why are you making that face?

DEE   He was just – ugh god.

       They chink glasses and sip. SAM loves this.

SAM   I'll drink to that.

       DEE smiles.

       He knew about wine though?

DEE   Oh yes. On our first date we got in an argument in a restaurant because I really liked the wine we were drinking and he said it was corked. So we got the waiter to come over and taste it and he practically vomited.

       They laugh.

       You'd get us any old shit from Tescos, didn't you?

SAM   Well we were saving to buy a house.

DEE   God if you could build a house on empty wine bottles.

SAM   We'd have had a MANSION.

       SAM looks at her.

       So that's done now with him is it?

DEE   Over.

       SAM nods.

       Liking yourself when you're with someone is half of the love affair.

SAM	Now that's very profound. You've obviously learned how to READ in the big city. And you didn't like yourself when you were with him?
DEE	Nooo.
SAM	Why not?
DEE	I came out weird.
SAM	Like how?

DEE *shrugs*.

DEE	You wouldn't have recognised me.
SAM	Why not?
DEE	I encouraged him to boss me around.
SAM	And then you didn't like it. What is that with you?
DEE	What do you mean?

SAM	What else?
DEE	He always took the bigger half.
SAM	I'm gonna kill him.

Kat's done that.

DEE	What a bitc–
SAM	But her mum's ill so I can't say anything.
DEE	Damn. What was it?
SAM	Doughnut.
DEE	Ouch.
SAM	There was no jam in my bit at all.

DEE *shakes her head*.

| DEE | I had that with a croissant. I would just watch him every time, thinking I didn't see. But I did see. |

SAM   Everyone sees. (*Upset*.) They just don't care.

DEE   Have you ever fisted a girl?

SAM   What!?

DEE   I've decided to be more open sexually.

SAM   You can't ask me that.

DEE   You've come all the way down from Wales to fix my toilet. You obviously want some serious conversation. So have you?

SAM   No.

DEE   Why do you say it like that?

SAM   Just doesn't sound very pleasant.

DEE   It's not... unpleasant...

SAM   Is there a charming man I'm about to meet?

DEE   Or woman.

SAM   Really? Didn't see that coming.

       DEE *smiles*.

       You're so proud.

DEE   Does it turn you on?

SAM   (*Re: a tool*.) Could you hold that?

DEE   We never talked about turn-ons much did we?

SAM   Could you hold that?

SAM *passes her the tool and then goes back into the bathroom.*

He cranks something.

I can't do it, it's jammed, the whole thing.

DEE   Is that my fault?

SAM   It would serve you right if it was, but nope. It's been broke a while.

DEE   Bruck.
What do I do?

SAM   You'll have to call a real plumber.

DEE   Okay, and what do I do in the meantime?

SAM   Well, you've clearly been pissing in the shower.

DEE   Haven't.

He comes out. He shrugs a bit.

Thank you for trying.

SAM   S'alright. I actually feel sort of guilty towards you.

DEE   Towards me?

SAM   I thought you'd blocked it on purpose and you clearly haven't.

DEE   You thought I'd blocked it on purpose? For what possible reason?

SAM   Doesn't matter.

DEE   Oh, no, excellent, you thought I wanted to drag you all the way from Cardiff so I could gaze at your flattering boiler suit while you fished around my U-bend and pretended to know what a plumber does?

SAM   I do know what a plumber *does*.

DEE   And you thought I'd given up shitting and
           wadged up my only facilities in the hope of
           a quickie with you.

SAM   I just thought you were lonely.

DEE   What's wrong with Kat's mum?

SAM   Big C.

DEE   Oof. Where?

SAM   Swansea.

DEE   God. Dead within the month then?

           Sorry. That was horrible.

SAM   It's okay. It turns everyone horrible.

DEE   Is it turning Kat horrible?

           SAM *nods*.

           Is Kat being a dick? Want to talk about it? I can
           take it.

           He puts his head in his hands and rubs it.

SAM   Feel like I'm betraying her telling you this.

DEE   Telling me what?

           He laughs.

SAM   God I'm a bastard.
           My eczema's going as well because you're
           winding me up.

DEE   It's okay.

SAM   Yes. She's being... hard.

          I can't – don't know how to talk about it. My
          mouth won't actually...

          He mimes something coming out of his mouth.

DEE   So it's about sex, then?

          *He looks at her immediately embarrassed, then
          puts his head in his hands again. She pours herself
          some more wine and now pours him some.*

          It is SO painful that the first time you actually ever
          want to talk about sex with me is when it's about
          you shagging someone else.

SAM   I'm sorry, I'm a knob.

DEE   It's okay. My vagina's ears are burning. We're
          here for you.

SAM   I can't –

DEE   Just do it.

          Do you want me to ease you in?

          He still has his head in his hands.

          'Nipples.'

          *He doesn't move, just slightly puts his hands over
          his ears.*

          'Taking someone from behind.'

          He laughs in the same position.

          'Handjob.'

SAM   Okay. Okay.

          Did we not talk about sex once?

DEE   I never had the slightest idea what was going on in your head.

SAM   And that's just as it should be.

That's why they're called 'thoughts'.

SAM smiles at her glibly.

DEE   Okay. You did say ONE sexy thing once.

SAM   (*Hopefully.*) Did I?

DEE   Yeah.

SAM   What?

DEE   'Take your skirt off, baby.'

SAM reacts like he doesn't remember.

I'd just come home from work and I was in my coat. I walked into the living room. You were sitting on the sofa staring at the TV, and you barely looked at me as you said, 'Take your skirt off, baby.' You were fiddling with the remote and I could feel the electricity passing through me as I wondered what you were going to do. I knew that whatever it was, I was up to it. I slid my coat off my shoulders and let it drop to the floor. You still didn't look at me. I dropped the skirt. And the rest. Right then and there. You beckoned me to the sofa. I walked towards you, completely naked. You turned to me as I approached, raised your hand and –

SAM   – Handed you your jogging bottoms, yes I remember it was a movie night and they were straight out of the tumble dryer. Fuck.

He's laughing.

DEE   Hm.

SAM   I never really understood why you got
        COMPLETELY naked.

DEE   Yeah well.

        He's pissing himself.

SAM   You were walking SO slowly towards me.
        I remember!! I thought it was the creepiest thing.

DEE   Fuck off.

SAM   It was November. It was so cold. This is the best
        thing you've ever told me.

        He's still laughing.

DEE   Oh right, yeah, laugh it up, I'm ridiculous.

SAM   Take your skirt off, baby.

        SAM *chuckles.*

DEE   Great. Good one.

        SAM *stops laughing suddenly.*

        What?

        SAM *stares at her.*

        Katya Mendoza – there I said her whole name.

        Sam.

SAM *starts to kiss her passionately.*

A fly is unzipped.

Is this okay?

SAM   Yeah.

DEE   I want you so much.

SAM   Shh.

DEE   Ahh – ow.

SAM   Sorry –

DEE   Maybe get –

SAM   Mm?

DEE   There's some um – stuff in the drawer there.

SAM *scrabbles. He finds a bottle of lube as they're kissing. He squeezes it. And squeezes it.*

SAM   It's empty.

DEE *looks up at him.* SAM *looks really embarrassed, horrified.*

They both laugh.

16. Miles 5

MILES *and* DEE *as before*.

MILES   'It'? Delilah?

DEE   Yeah.

MILES   Say the word.

DEE   Domination.

MILES   Say the word.

DEE   Spanking.

DEE *grins, trying not to giggle*. MILES *sits back and looks at her*.

MILES   Why do you want to know what it feels like?

DEE   Because – it's taboo…?

MILES   That's not a reason.

DEE   Yes it is.

MILES   Specifically.

DEE *shrugs*.

DEE   It's a fantasy I suppose.

I always wondered if I'd like it.

And then I thought fuckit.

MILES   Answer the question.

DEE   I don't fucking know.

MILES *raises an eyebrow*. DEE *smiles*.

I suppose I feel – Oh GOD. Not like I need it, I don't need anything.

I thought it might turn me on.

MILES Why?

DEE Why.
Exactly.
I didn't have a weird upbringing, my mum didn't
only talk to me when she was having a poo –

MILES What?

DEE That's – that's a theory for why people get in to
poo sex.
Because their mum / only talked to them when –

MILES When she was –

DEE Going for a poo, yeah.

Like – they associate poo with love and attention.

MILES Oh.

DEE Probably just a busy mum.

MILES God.

DEE I know, yeah.

MILES Gross.

DEE (*Laughs*.) Don't be so judgey!

MILES I'm not – but –

DEE You of all people.

    What's in this for you?

MILES Not doing that.

DEE Are you ashamed of it?

MILES   No.

DEE   Why not?
         You get off on being violent to women.

MILES   I'm not going down this rabbit hole.

DEE   Why is it a rabbit hole, because you can't answer
         the question?

MILES   I give women what they want.

DEE   And what do you get out of it?
         Dominating women?

         Are you terrified of me, Miles?

         Maybe you're not so surprising.

MILES   Go on.

DEE   Well –

MILES   Get it all out.

DEE   Maybe that's why you don't like 'woolly liberals'.

MILES   Okay.

DEE   Because they question the status quo.

MILES   Excellent, and?

DEE   They make you feel judged.

MILES   And?

DEE   And maybe you should be judged

MILES   Well that's not very broad-minded of them, is it?

         It's consensual.

DEE   So?

MILES   *Everything*.

DEE   Don't you question your sexual psyche?

MILES   All the time.

            Is this just about sex for you?

DEE   I could ask you the same –

MILES   Well I asked it first.

DEE   I – get turned on – by bossy men.

MILES   Does that bother you?

DEE   It doesn't sit well with my feminism, Miles.

17. Sam 2

Twenty minutes after the last scene. SAM *and* DEE *have just had sex.*

She hands him the bin and he puts the condom in it. Does himself up. She goes into the bathroom.

SAM   Just turn up at an estate agent, tell them what you want, pick a flat, pack your stuff and go.

DEE   It's miles from being as easy as that.

SAM   You're dithering. As usual. You'll feel so much happier in a nice place, you'll be proud of yourself.

DEE   I have a shit credit rating.

SAM   Have you even checked, I bet it's not that bad.

DEE   I bet it is.

SAM   Am I mansplaining to you now?

DEE   I didn't say that.

       DEE *leans out of the bathroom, raises an eyebrow. She hands him a wet wipe.*

SAM   Thank you.

       He wipes his hands and stomach. She is wiping her hands too.

DEE   Can we talk about that?

SAM   Yeah.

DEE   I was a bit different was I?

SAM   Nah it was good.

DEE   Well I – What you doing?

        SAM *is playing on the stepper exercise machine.*

SAM   This new is it?

DEE   I can't afford the gym any more.

SAM   You're trying to lose weight?

DEE   I'm cutting out sugar with Paul McKenna.

SAM   Could you not just give up sugar on your –

DEE   No it can only be done with Paul McKenna's help,
        the back of the book was very clear about that.

        SAM *smiles. She smiles back.*

SAM   Has someone made you feel bad about your body?

        DEE *shrugs.*

        I need a piss.

DEE   We could go out somewhere. Have lunch.

SAM   In the shower is it?

DEE   I would go on your knees, to avoid the old –
        splashback.

SAM   Right.

        He goes into the bathroom. He gets on his knees.

        He stands.

        That's not happening.

        He comes out zipping his flies.

DEE   Shall we go out for lunch, Sam?

SAM   Have you got anything to eat in the house?

DEE   Um –

SAM   I might go get a kebab.

         DEE *wrinkles her nose.*

DEE   What, a shaved one?

SAM   Do you want anything?

DEE   The shaved one?

SAM   Do you want anything?

DEE   No thank you.

         SAM *starts to walk towards the door, then he
         turns slowly around and faces her.*

SAM   She's – different. I don't know.

DEE   What?

SAM   I don't know, she seems to be being brutally blunt
         about stuff – weird stuff and saying some things
         that are a bit out there that she probably doesn't
         even mean. Stuff you can't really take back. And
         I'm a bit knocked for six –

DEE   Like –

SAM   Like well she said she was faking. Basically. All
         the orgasms I've ever given her.

DEE   She –

SAM   Yeah, like, she's got into a rhythm of faking all her
         orgasms when we're together, she's been doing it
         since before we met, and she's still doing it now,

and although she enjoys sex with me, she's not
actually – what I'm doing doesn't actually – get
her there. And it never has.

DEE   Wow.

SAM   It's killed me to be honest.

DEE   Yeah, it would do.

SAM   I just – I needed to see you because –

I can't fucking go near her at the moment.

DEE   Is she distraught?

SAM   She's different…

We're like ghosts a bit.

DEE   Still, her mum's dying, so –

SAM   She's been lying to me for our whole relationship.

You never did this to me, did you?

DEE   No.

18. Vera 5

VERA *and* DEE *are in bed.* DEE *is asleep.* VERA *has glasses on and is opening and reading and sorting* DEE*'s mail and bills. She is highlighting things and using her phone as a calculator. It is morning. They are both in their pyjamas. There is a sound at the door.* VERA *watches the door. It opens.* EDDIE *walks in with a pathetic bunch of new flowers.*

He sees VERA, *sitting up, staring directly at him.*

EDDIE   Oh... uuh... oh...

             They keep staring at each other. DEE *sleeps unaware.*

             I've come to... um...

VERA   Drop off your keys?

EDDIE   Yes.

             He backs out of the door, leaving them on the floor.

             I knew it by the way.

             He leaves.

             DEE *wakes up. Looks at* VERA.

DEE   Hey. You stayed?

VERA   Yes.

DEE   Aw. (*Jumping out of bed.*) OH MY GOD WHAT IS THE TIME?

VERA   Saturday.

DEE   (*Back into bed.*) Oh thank god.

VERA   Breakfast?

DEE   I have eggs in the fruit bowl in the fridge.

             VERA *gets up and goes to the fridge. She turns round to* DEE.

VERA   We could do this you know?

DEE   What?

VERA   You and me.

DEE   Did I touch you up last night?

VERA   (*Laughs*.) No.

DEE   I had the filthiest dream.

VERA   Lucky. I dreamt of rocks eating other rocks again.

DEE   God that is horrendous.

VERA   Just loud.

         She rummages in the fridge again.

         So. You and me?

         This. We could do this properly... move in together, get a little two-bed flat.

         What?

DEE   I can't afford it.

VERA   You can actually.

DEE   No.

VERA   Yes you can, I opened your mail. You need to cancel a few things, move some stuff around but you should be fine.

DEE   You WHAT?!

VERA   Let me show you.

DEE	Vera, are you kidding me?
VERA	I knew you weren't gonna do it, so –
DEE	It's not your mail to open.
VERA	Don't you feel better now it's done?
DEE	What is it with people opening up my life, do I have the word 'twat' stapled to the back of my head?
VERA	I thought you needed help.
DEE	When I need help, I'll ask for it.

She looks round.

Did you tidy my flat while I was asleep? I knew where everything was.

Oh my god is that a fucking mousetrap?

VERA	It's a shithole.
DEE	Well if it's such a shithole, why can't I get some fucking PEACE around here?

(*About the mousetrap.*) These are inhumane.

VERA	I don't know, Dee, why can't you?
DEE	All I want is to do it myself. That's all I want
VERA	I think that's the last thing you want, babe.

So why did you call me last night then?

You think I've got endless free time?

DEE	Why did you come then?

| VERA | You know what? I have stuff to do in the office myself today so I'll see you around. |

DEE   Okay fine.

            VERA *gets ready to leave.*

VERA   I have done you a financial plan on your laptop.

19. Miles 6

The same as before.

MILES *is laughing.*

MILES   'It doesn't sit well with my feminism.'
            If I had a penny.

            Are you worried you're alone?
            You're not alone.

DEE   So you reckon you know other women who want
            – this stuff?

MILES   'This stuff.' Yes. Many.

DEE   Like who?

MILES   Busy, sexy, strong women like you.

DEE   Oh thanks.

MILES   They feel – guilty.

            I think.

            You're all made to feel guilty all the time.

DEE   By 'The Patriarchy'?

MILES   Well yeah. The media.

DEE   About what?

MILES   You know this.

            What you eat, how you look.

DEE   They want you to spank them because they've had a chocolate bar?

MILES   Yes.

DEE   That makes no sense.

MILES   It's not about sense.

            What do you feel guilty about?

DEE   I've made peace with it all.

MILES   What's all this about your 'feminism' then?

DEE   I've made peace with fucking everything mate.

MILES   In what way?

DEE   Just that I'm a fucking alien or something.

MILES   Why?

            DEE *shrugs*.

DEE   Do you think I'm a pervert?

            I always thought someone was just gonna come along and 'get' me.

MILES   Yeah no that's a fantasy.

            DEE *deflates. She sits*.

            I'm not going to do this if you're feeling weak. It's no fun for me.

DEE   What?

MILES   You have all the power here.

            Go ahead, call me a sadist. Call me a pervert.

DEE   You must get it all the time.

MILES   Hardly ever, actually.

           MILES *stands*.

DEE   Don't go.

MILES   You don't want me to go?

           DEE *shakes her head*.

           Well you've gotta lighten up then.

           Kink is not 'fucked up', Dee. Kink is fun. You find
           like-minded people, you play, you go home. I've
           seen every kind of person in this strange little
           community, they're all different, all in it for
           different reasons.

           Thing is, it's up to you what you do with your
           body, and it's up to you whether that defines you
           or not.

DEE   Okay.

MILES   You've got a complicated sexual appetite, that's a
           fine thing.

DEE   I can lighten up.

MILES   Oh you can, can you?

           She nods.

           Look at me.

           She does.

           Have you thought about this stuff a lot?

DEE   Yes.

MILES   Has it played a regular part in your sexual
           fantasies?

DEE   No.

MILES   Be honest.

DEE   Yes I've thought about it a lot, yes.

MILES   Well it's probably something you should try then.

             Now what happened to that hairbrush you were
             going to get for me?

DEE   Um – I – thought you brought your own – stuff.

             I've got the blow-drying ones – mainly.

             DEE *is trying not to smile*. MILES *is still
             convincingly looking confused. He stands.*
             DEE *takes a step back.*

MILES   Did you get one or didn't you?

DEE   No.

             MILES *leans forward towards her and smiles.*

MILES   No what?

DEE   No sir?

MILES   Miles will do.

             DEE *smiles.*

DEE   No, Miles.

             MILES *smiles. He takes her hand.*

20. Sam 3

Two weeks later.

SAM *and* DEE *stand in her room.*

SAM   How's your toilet?

DEE   Fixed.

SAM   No thanks to me.

DEE   You tried.

SAM   You overpaid me.

DEE   Well, I've still got a job.

           For three more weeks.

SAM   Did they tell you that?

DEE   I found out.

SAM   Are you sure?

DEE   One of the interns is the nephew of the CEO.

SAM   And he told you?

DEE   Took great pleasure in it.

SAM   So you're coming home then?

DEE   I'm trying to get some interviews.

SAM   Up here?

DEE   Yeah.

           How was the funeral?

SAM   What do you mean, how was it?

DEE   Was it sad?

SAM   No we booked a comedian, so it was fine, actually.

           DEE *laughs a bit*.

           Were you off out were you?

DEE   It's alright.

           DEE *sends a text*.

           How's Kat?

SAM   Um.
           Difficult.
           I get it, it's bad enough with her mum.

DEE   Yeah.

SAM   But –

           It's hard.

DEE   Yeah.

SAM   I'm moving out.

DEE   With Kat?

SAM   Nah, let her have the house. Fancy a new start.
           Thought I might move up here.

DEE   Up to London?

SAM   Thought maybe you might want a housemate.

DEE   What?

SAM   I thought maybe you might want a housemate.

DEE   You thought we should move in together?

SAM   Yeah. Why not. Be cheaper. Good company.

DEE   As in me and you?

SAM   That's what I'm saying.

        DEE *smiles.* SAM *smiles. Then she stops.*

DEE   We couldn't live together. Without.

SAM   Without sleeping together?
        Don't worry about that.
        I have a feeling things might go your way.

        SAM *oikishly hums and rocks an imaginary baby.*

DEE   Oh.

SAM   I've started to look at them differently in the
        street.

DEE   You can get arrested for that.

        He grabs her.

SAM   Fuckit!

        He indicates the window.

        C'mon, there must be some less 'London-y' places
        we could find?

        Richmond, by the river?

DEE   Yeah.

SAM   (*Like a joke.*) Or you could just bloody come back
          to Swansea.

DEE   I could.

          SAM *cocks his head and gives her a 'look'. He
          makes a sound like they're both getting convinced
          about it.*

          Mmm…

SAM   To get an actual house, that we own, instead of
          a shoebox in the sky.

          DEE *smiles.*

          We're waiting for you.
          The girls all miss you.

DEE   I've barely spoken to them.

SAM   Exactly! They miss you like crazy.
          We've all missed you, and fuck 'em if *they*
          haven't.
          I've missed you.

          Just come home darling.

DEE   Okay.

SAM   Okay?! Okay! Oh baby!

          We're gonna be so fucking happy. We'll have
          a house, and – and a cat… You hate cats. No cats.
          Kat can keep the cat.

          Babies!
          We'll get it sorted.
          I'm ready.

          DEE *grins and nods.*

          Ahh my sweet girl! There she is!

He goes to hold DEE, *but she takes a step back.*

DEE   Does she know you want to break up with her?

SAM   Who?

Well I didn't know what you were gonna say, so –

DEE *nods slowly.*

What's up?

DEE   Nothing – I just.

SAM *embraces her.*

Nothing.

21. Vera 6

Awkward pause. DEE *is bouncing on the bed nervously.*

VERA   I leave you alone for a whole week, and now I can't keep up.

DEE   I know.

I wanted to call you but I didn't know –

VERA   This Miles was from a *website*?!

DEE *nods.*

A special…?

DEE   A fetish website, yeah.

VERA   Will you do it again?

DEE   Honestly, it was *amazing*.

VERA   Really?

DEE   Super-hot.

         DEE *nods*. VERA *nods*.

         A lot of women are in to it.

VERA   In to being hit, are they?

DEE   Well – it's complicated but – yeah. It has nothing
         to do with who you are.

VERA   How can it have nothing to do with who you are?

DEE   Is this grossing you out?

VERA   No.

DEE   So what's up with you?

         VERA *is dragging some clothes up from under*
         DEE*'s feet and starts tidying up.*

VERA   Why do you live like this?

         The cesspit.

DEE   I thrive in it.

VERA   Come on.

DEE   Don't you judge me as well.

VERA   As well as what?

DEE   All / the men.

VERA   All your men exactly. Who treat you like a *baby*.

DEE   What?

VERA   What is wrong with you?

DEE   Sex is different.

VERA   Why is it different?

DEE   I suppose only a deeply respectful fuck turns
you on?

VERA   You fetishise your own self-loathing.

DEE   Just because I'm different to you –

VERA   Not different. Disrespectful.
To yourself.

I hate it.

DEE   You hate me?

VERA   No. You hate you.
Let's talk about that.

DEE   Look – kink is – / actually very respectful.

VERA   I don't care about your kinky shit. I mean the rest
of it.

DEE   The rest of what?

VERA   You are responsible for your own happiness.

She shrugs.

DEE   What, are *you* happy?

VERA   I don't care so much.

DEE   About *happiness*?

VERA   About being alone.

DEE   Well then you're very unusual.

VERA   These men.

DEE   What?

VERA   They're not good enough for you.

DEE   Well that's no fucking good to me, is it?

         Sam wants me back.

VERA   Sam?

DEE   Yes. And I'm moving back to Swansea to be
         with him.
         My job's supposed to be over this week and
         they've given me no indication they're keeping
         me on. So.

VERA   When are you going?

DEE   Next weekend.
         He's coming to pick me up.

         VERA *is looking more and more furious.*

VERA   Why are you back in touch with him?

DEE   Because he came up to see me.

VERA   Why?

DEE   To fix my toilet.

VERA   Is he a plumber now?

DEE   No. He couldn't fix it.

VERA   He came to tell you he loved you?

DEE   Yes.

VERA   That it's over with his girlfriend?

DEE   Yes.

VERA   Since her mum has died?

         He came to ask you back?

         To start a life with him in Swansea?

         Because he loves you?

DEE   Yes.

VERA   You must be very happy.

DEE   Don't give me that, okay.

         At least I actually have relationships.
         At least I trust people.

VERA   You don't know shit about that.
         You don't know anything about my dating
         experiences.
         How they see me, how they speak to me.
         You are part of a mainstream.
         You don't have a clue what it's like to be me.

DEE   Well you never tell me.

VERA   You never ask!
         I could tell you all about my stupid shit dates, but
         you never really ask.

And you know why? Because I'm not a *fucking man*. So you're not that interested.

If you wanna know, I could beat myself up about that this person who doesn't want me.
That they're happy to sleep with me when they're feeling lonely, but they're ultimately not interested.

I've even tried to change myself for that person but it didn't work and I'm not going to do it any more.

DEE   Oh my god I can't believe you have someone.
You've had a whole life outside this flat and I don't know anything about it.

VERA   Or you could say that I've had a whole life inside this flat and you know everything about it.

It's alright.

DEE   Vera – I –

VERA   I'm over it.

But why did you come here?
To go home again?

You think it makes no difference to people?

I don't know whether that's arrogant or humble.

Either way, it's insulting.

DEE   Vera –

VERA *leaves.*

22. Miles, Paddy and Eddie

Time passes. DEE *tidies up a bit. She opens her mail.*

The voices of MILES, EDDIE *and* PADDY *come into* DEE*'s space. As she tidies and sorts, she answers them without looking at them.*

MILES   Is the lady of the house taking visitors?

DEE   Oh hi.

MILES   I thought I might pop by and see whether you'd
            ever seen a ropey old French film called *The Story
            of O*.

EDDIE   Dee.

DEE   Eddie?

EDDIE   Don't freak out.
            I left my keys here

DEE   Did you, fuck.

EDDIE   No I did.

MILES   And I thought you might fancy some company.

DEE   Why?

EDDIE   Because Vera shouted at me.

MILES   Because we had a good time.

DEE   Alright.

MILES   And I don't like to think of you up here alone.

DEE   It's weirdly not as lonely as you'd think.

PADDY   Delilah!

            A sound of a stone hits a window.

DEE   What the fuck?
            Paddy you'll break the window!

PADDY   Nice to see you too.

EDDIE   *She's* not here again is she?

DEE   No.

EDDIE   Your *girlfriend*.

DEE   She's not either of those things.

EDDIE   Why not, she's always here?

          DEE *picks up her mobile. She makes a call.*

PADDY   I was wondering why you weren't in / work.

EDDIE   I was wondering about your plans for this weekend.

DEE   I'm moving back to Wales.

EDDIE   What?

MILES   What?

PADDY   You what?

MILES   You can't do that.

DEE   Why not?

MILES   You live here now.

DEE   Yeah, with no job.

          (*Speaks to her mobile.*) Pick up the phone.

PADDY   Who says you have no job?

DEE   You said –

PADDY   Yeah well, turns out I'm a little gobshite.

DEE   What do you mean?

PADDY   Turns out the *laydees* in your office who you're always slagging off, bloody love you.

          Plus Uncle Bryan owes me big from Glasto, so.

DEE   Blimey.

          DEE *is still making a call on her mobile.*

          Pick up the phone.

PADDY   Are you calling for drugs?

MILES   Got somewhere to be?

DEE   I'm just – calling a friend.

EDDIE   Vera?

DEE   Yes! Have you taken your keys yet?

EDDIE   Alright!

PADDY   *I'm* your friend.

MILES   You're distracted.

DEE   Just let me see if she answers.

            EDDIE *appears*.

EDDIE   Send the old cow my love.
            I'll call you soon, kitten. Augh. Still *cute*.

            EDDIE *kisses her and leaves*.

            PADDY *appears*.

PADDY   Fine I get the hint. Get your arse to the office on
            Monday. Or I'll cry.

            PADDY *kisses her and leaves*.

            DEE *dials the phone again*.

            MILES *appears*.

MILES   I don't think she's answering, darling.

            DEE *puts the phone down*.

            Are you really moving back?

            DEE *nods*.

DEE   Any minute.

MILES   Shame.

            I brought you another little present, but it sounds
            like it's not the right time.

DEE   Well, he's gonna be here –

             SAM *appears. At the same time,* MILES *pulls out a wooden hairbrush and hands it to her.*

MILES   (*To* SAM.) Oh. Hi.

             (*To* DEE.) Thanks for letting me borrow it.

             DEE *takes the hairbrush and smiles at* MILES *as he leaves.*

23. Sam 4

SAM *and* DEE *are alone in the flat. Everyone else has gone.*

SAM   He was your neighbour, was he?

DEE   Yeah.

             No.

             He was –

SAM   I don't wanna know, darling.

             Thought you'd at least have started packing.

DEE   Barely had a chance.

             Let's do it now, shall we?

             She starts chucking things into a massive bag. SAM *watches her. He scans the room nervously.*

SAM   You wanna go *tonight*?

DEE   Yep. I called up Morgan Hotels. Happy to have me back straight away.

SAM   Oh good.

DEE   I can start on Monday.

           What's wrong?

SAM   I thought this was sorted. Me and you.

DEE   It is.

SAM   We've had our fun, now.
           Back to normal.

           I thought that's what you wanted.

           DEE *slows down packing and looks at him.*

           Who was that guy?

DEE   He was a friend.

SAM   He's not your *friend*. You barely know him.

DEE   I've been here eight months.

SAM   Exactly. You've proven your point.

           SAM *smiles glibly and flexes his muscles.*

           Have you been working out?

           Doing steroids with the lads, like.

           I can't do it too much, it makes you infertile.
           You'll never forgive me if we can't have babies.

           Or maybe you're still on about not wanting them?

           You are ridiculous.

           Wow.

You'll change your mind.

Look I get it alright, we've had some time, I'm a bit different, you're a lot different, but I'm talking about *us* now.

DEE   I know.

SAM   Some things are precious.

DEE   I know that.

SAM   Don't fuck this.

DEE   What do you mean, don't fuck this? Why is it all on me?

SAM   What?

DEE   Why am I quitting my job?

SAM   Excuse me?

DEE   Why do I have to move?

SAM   You don't live here.

DEE   I do actually.

Why do I have to come to Swansea?

SAM   It doesn't have to be Swansea.

DEE   *Really*?

SAM   We can go anywhere you like.

DEE   As long as we're together?

SAM   Yes.

DEE   Kensington Olympia?

SAM   Maybe.

DEE   You'd give up your business for me?

SAM   If I have to.

DEE   You can say that though, can't you?
        Because you know I would never ever ask.

        Why are you doing this?

SAM   Doing what?

DEE   Why me?

SAM   I love you, alright? I have the feeling called 'love'.

DEE   But what is it about me?

SAM   Darling –

DEE   Just have a bash.

SAM   You're lovely, aren't you?

DEE   Wasn't Kat lovely?

SAM   Yeah but.

DEE   Why me again, all of a sudden?

SAM   I can't do this / sort of chat.

DEE   Try.

SAM   It's not 'all of a sudden'.

        It's not been the same since you left.

        You had standards.

DEE   What does that mean?

SAM   You were hopeful.
         It was nice.
         Made me feel different about myself.
         Like there was more.

         Is that enough?

DEE   How is Kat, by the way?

SAM   Why d'you keep asking me that?

DEE   I can just imagine, you telling everyone from home.
         (*In his voice.*) 'I cannot deal with her, but I'll still
         be there for her, like.'
         And you'll be the hero, and she'll be alone.

         And you can tell her from me that if she's feeling
         a bit crushed by that experience, she can come and
         hang out with me.

SAM   What are you on about now?

         Are you coming home?

         Jesus.

         Are you seriously saying you'd rather be here in
         this fucked situation with this fucked-up flat and
         your weird friends than be home with me?

         DEE *nods*.

         SAM *starts to cry*.

DEE *comes behind him. He starts.*

The mouse scuttles out.

JESUS!

DEE   It's alright!

SAM   It's a fucking mouse Dee! You're fucking infested! You can't live here!

DEE   It's alright.

SAM   What the fuck is going on?!

DEE   It's alright! It's just a mouse.

        SAM *is shaking, holding himself. He pulls his legs up on the bed, fearfully.*

SAM   God.

DEE   Are you okay?

        He laughs a bit.

        You're shaking.

SAM   I could do with a drink.

DEE   Shall we go out?

SAM   What?
        Haven't you got any in?

DEE   Um –

        She checks the fridge.

SAM   It's all you Londoners do isn't it? Necking booze in the daytime.

DEE   I'm out.

SAM   Wow.

DEE   We could –

SAM   It's alright. I'll pop and get us some beers.

DEE   Are you sure?

SAM   Yeah.

         See you in a minute then. We'll talk it through,
         we'll be fine. Alright?

         Alright, woman?

         He looks at her meaningfully.

         She nods.

         He kisses her cheek. He leaves.

         After a few beats, DEE *grabs her bag. She puts
         her bag on the bed. She stares at it. She makes a
         call. As the call is answered, she breathes a sigh of
         relief. She grabs her bag and goes to leave the flat.*

DEE   Vera.

         Blackout.

         The End.

Other Titles in this Series

Annie Baker
THE FLICK

Mike Bartlett
BULL
GAME
AN INTERVENTION
KING CHARLES III
WILD

Jez Butterworth
THE FERRYMAN
JERUSALEM
JEZ BUTTERWORTH PLAYS: ONE
MOJO
THE NIGHT HERON
PARLOUR SONG
THE RIVER
THE WINTERLING

Caryl Churchill
BLUE HEART
CHURCHILL PLAYS: THREE
CHURCHILL PLAYS: FOUR
CHURCHILL: SHORTS
CLOUD NINE
DING DONG THE WICKED
A DREAM PLAY *after* Strindberg
DRUNK ENOUGH TO SAY
    I LOVE YOU?
ESCAPED ALONE
FAR AWAY
HERE WE GO
HOTEL
ICECREAM
LIGHT SHINING IN
    BUCKINGHAMSHIRE
LOVE AND INFORMATION
MAD FOREST
A NUMBER
PIGS AND DOGS
SEVEN JEWISH CHILDREN
THE SKRIKER
THIS IS A CHAIR
THYESTES *after* Seneca
TRAPS

debbie tucker green
BORN BAD
DIRTY BUTTERFLY
HANG
NUT
A PROFOUNDLY AFFECTIONATE,
    PASSIONATE DEVOTION TO
    SOMEONE (– *NOUN*)
RANDOM
STONING MARY
TRADE & GENERATIONS
TRUTH AND RECONCILIATION

Vivienne Franzmann
BODIES
MOGADISHU
PESTS
THE WITNESS

James Fritz
THE FALL
ROSS & RACHEL

Sam Holcroft
COCKROACH
DANCING BEARS
EDGAR & ANNABEL
PINK
RULES FOR LIVING
THE WARDROBE
WHILE YOU LIE

Vicky Jones
THE ONE

Anna Jordan
CHICKEN SHOP
FREAK
YEN

Lucy Kirkwood
BEAUTY AND THE BEAST
    with Katie Mitchell
BLOODY WIMMIN
THE CHILDREN
CHIMERICA
HEDDA *after* Ibsen
IT FELT EMPTY WHEN THE
    HEART WENT AT FIRST BUT
    IT IS ALRIGHT NOW
LUCY KIRKWOOD PLAYS: ONE
MOSQUITOES
NSFW
TINDERBOX

Clare McIntyre
LOW LEVEL PANIC
MY HEART'S A SUITCASE
    & LOW LEVEL PANIC
THE MATHS TUTOR
THE THICKNESS OF SKIN

Nina Raine
CONSENT
RABBIT
TIGER COUNTRY
TRIBES

Stef Smith
GIRL IN THE MACHINE
HUMAN ANIMALS
REMOTE
SWALLOW

Sam Steiner
LEMONS LEMONS LEMONS
    LEMONS LEMONS

Jack Thorne
2ND MAY 1997
BUNNY
BURYING YOUR BROTHER IN
    THE PAVEMENT
HOPE
JACK THORNE PLAYS: ONE
LET THE RIGHT ONE IN
    after John Ajvide Lindqvist
MYDIDAE
THE SOLID LIFE OF SUGAR WATER
STACY & FANNY AND FAGGOT
WHEN YOU CURE ME
WOYZECK *after* Büchner

Phoebe Waller-Bridge
FLEABAG

'A great published script makes you understand what the play is, at its heart' *Slate Magazine*

Enjoyed this book? Choose from hundreds more classic and contemporary plays from Nick Hern Books, the UK's leading independent theatre publisher.

Our full range is available to browse online now, including:

Award-winning plays from leading contemporary dramatists, including *King Charles III* by Mike Bartlett, *Anne Boleyn* by Howard Brenton, *Jerusalem* by Jez Butterworth, *A Breakfast of Eels* by Robert Holman, *Chimerica* by Lucy Kirkwood, *The Night Alive* by Conor McPherson, *The James Plays* by Rona Munro, *Nell Gwynn* by Jessica Swale, and many more...

Ground-breaking drama from the most exciting up-and-coming playwrights, including Vivienne Franzmann, James Fritz, Ella Hickson, Anna Jordan, Jack Thorne, Phoebe Waller-Bridge, Tom Wells, and many more...

Twentieth-century classics, including *Cloud Nine* by Caryl Churchill, *Death and the Maiden* by Ariel Dorfman, *Pentecost* by David Edgar, *Angels in America* by Tony Kushner, *Long Day's Journey into Night* by Eugene O'Neill, *The Deep Blue Sea* by Terence Rattigan, *Machinal* by Sophie Treadwell, and many more...

Timeless masterpieces from playwrights throughout the ages, including Anton Chekhov, Euripides, Henrik Ibsen, Federico García Lorca, Christopher Marlowe, Molière, William Shakespeare, Richard Brinsley Sheridan, Oscar Wilde, and many more...

Every playscript is a world waiting to be explored. Find yours at **www.nickhernbooks.co.uk** – you'll receive a 20% discount, plus free UK postage & packaging for orders over £30.

'Publishing plays gives permanent form to an evanescent art, and allows many more people to have some kind of experience of a play than could ever see it in the theatre' *Nick Hern, publisher*

www.nickhernbooks.co.uk

A Nick Hern Book

Touch first published in Great Britain in 2017 as a paperback original by
Nick Hern Books Limited, The Glasshouse, 49a Goldhawk Road, London W12 8QP,
in association with Soho Theatre and DryWrite

Touch copyright © 2017 Vicky Jones

Cover photograph by Matt Crockett

Designed and typeset by Nick Hern Books, London
Printed in Great Britain by CPI Books (UK) Ltd

A CIP catalogue record for this book is available from the British Library

ISBN 978 1 84842 695 5